KIRANAWALA
KIRANA RETAILER OF INDIA

BALWANT SINGH RANA

Unsung Heroes of India's Economic Backbone

In honour of the **12 million Kirana retailers** who enrich the vast expanse of India, this book is a tribute to the unsung heroes of our nation. These hardworking and determined individuals are the foundation of India's retail world, making a significant impact on the national economy. With steadfast dedication, they have become a powerful force, contributing an impressive **10% to the country's GDP** and p**roviding 8% of the nation's employment.** The Kiranawala, also known as Kirana retailers, are not merely shopkeepers; they are the keepers of tradition, sustainability, and community values.

Their modest and simple shops are the true essence of Indian retail, functioning as lively centres for trade and human connection. Acknowledging their vital role, this book explores the detailed world of Kirana retail, revealing their struggles, victories, and the rich fabric of their stories. This is a celebration of their unyielding spirit and an effort to shed light on their crucial role in our society's structure. This book is dedicated with sincere gratitude to the Kiranawala, who continue to serve our communities with commitment and pride.

Kiranaawala, the backbone of the country | Kiranaawala, an integral part of every household | Kiranaawala, the heartbeat of the community | Kiranaawala, the guardians of tradition |Kiranaawala, the soul of India.

--==--

Contents

Foreword

Foreword by Mr. Pawan Sharma, Proprietor of Kalpatru Departmental Store, Jagatpura, Jaipur

I, Pawan Sharma, have been steering my retail venture named Kalpataru Store for the past two decades in the vibrant city of Jaipur, alongside my life partner. However, when I reflect on the current state of affairs in the business landscape and compare it with the situation of the last 8-10 years, a distressing observation emerges – the plight of small retail shopkeepers has reached a precarious juncture.

The realm of small retail is contracting, leading some shopkeepers to shutter their establishments and resort to earning meager wages ranging from Rs 10,000 to Rs 15,000. The question that arises is: What transpired in these 8-10 years that brought small traders to their knees?

Upon introspection of the past decade, I discerned three primary reasons contributing to the decline of small shopkeepers, pushing contemporary small businessmen toward destitution. One of these factors is the evolving landscape of technology. A decade ago, customers used to procure their goods by physically visiting the store or submitting their monthly ration lists to the shopkeeper for home delivery. Presently, with mobile accessibility and numerous purchasing apps, customers can order items from the comfort of their homes, receiving deliveries within minutes.

The second factor is the pervasive influence of marketing on our minds. Technology has ensnared customers in the web of false marketing claims. The ubiquity of mobile devices has made individuals so occupied that stepping out of the house becomes undesirable. There is little time for comparing the weight, MRP, and quality of goods; individuals tend to accept what advertisements portray as true, oblivious to the possibility that discounts, free items, and home delivery may come at a higher hidden cost.

The third major factor is the adverse impact of monetary funding. Around 8-10 years ago, when an individual opened a shop, they would commence their business by investing personal capital, earning modest profits to sustain their livelihood. However, in the present scenario, due to both indigenous and foreign funding, online companies and malls attract consumers by offering some products at a lower cost, or by packaging items with higher MRP and lower weight than the manufacturing companies, leading to deceptive practices.

While technology has undoubtedly bestowed certain conveniences upon us, it has concurrently given rise to challenges. The evolving business landscape, while facilitating consumers with the convenience of home-based shopping and delivery, has also engendered a sense of lethargy among consumers. False marketing claims have further exacerbated the situation, causing individuals to perceive right as wrong and wrong as right.

I implore my fellow business associates to adapt their business strategies to the changing times by embracing technology. By doing so, we can fortify our presence in the market and enlighten consumers about the veracity of marketing claims.

Furthermore, if governments universally implement the rule of one weight, one MRP across the entire country, even small shopkeepers can adequately meet the needs of their families. This approach would enable them to revive the joy and happiness they once shared with their families.

Balwant Singh Rana, the esteemed author of this book, boasts extensive expertise in the Kirana retail sector. His commendable efforts to shed light on the challenges faced by Kirana retailers are truly praiseworthy. I anticipate that this book will serve as a valuable tool in fostering a deeper understanding of our significant contributions to individuals' lives and the overall GDP of our nation. Through Rana's insightful narrative, readers will gain insights into the crucial role played by Kirana retailers, recognizing the pivotal impact they have on both the personal experiences of individuals and the economic landscape of the country. It is a hopeful expectation that this literary endeavor will contribute to a broader appreciation of the vital role played by Kirana retailers in the fabric of our society and economy.

Foreword by Akshay Vijay, Proprietor of R.R. Departmental Store, Model Town, Jagatpura, Jaipur

As a Kirana retailer, my journey, much like that of my fellow Kirana retailers, has been both challenging and rewarding. The path of Kirana retail is not just a business; it is a lifelong pursuit that is deeply connected to our communities and our identities. It is a story of dreams, struggles, and a strong commitment to serving our neighbours and customers.

When I was first asked to contribute my insights to this book, I felt a mix of excitement and curiosity. What could a book really capture about our daily lives, the challenges we face, and the joys we experience as Kirana retailers? However, as I read through the pages, I found myself immersed in a narrative that deeply resonated with my own experiences, reflecting the feelings of many others in this profession.

What struck me the most about this book is how it captures the essence of Kirana retail – the difficulties, the triumphs, and the constant adaptation to an ever-changing world. It portrays our hardships, not as a burden, but as a testament to our resilience. Through this book, I felt connected to the stories of my fellow Kirana retailers across the country. Our experiences are shared, our challenges are the same, and our hopes and dreams are alike.

The hardships we face as Kirana retailers are unique. They stem from the daily grind, the financial pressures, the long hours, and the constant need to adapt. This book brings these feelings to life, acknowledging that our hardships are not a burden, but proof of our commitment to our businesses and our communities. It is the price we willingly pay to be the heart of our neighbourhoods.

As Kirana retailers, we often stand at the crossroads of tradition and modernity. We must uphold the values and connections that have defined Kirana stores for generations, while also embracing the digital age and adapting to the changing needs of our customers. This book does an excellent job of showing how technology, innovation, and a strong sense of tradition can go hand in hand.

What I truly appreciate about this book is its recognition of the Kirana store as more than just a place of commerce. It is a pillar of social unity. The book highlights the importance of community involvement, and how we are trusted friends and neighbours to those we serve. It reminds us that we are not just retailers; we are keepers of a tradition that brings people together.

The chapters on sustainability and social impact made me proud to see our role as advocates for environmentally responsible choices. The book acknowledges the efforts we make to stock locally sourced produce, reduce plastic use, and promote sustainable living – all of which align with the growing awareness of our customers about the environment.

This book not only resonated with my own experiences, but it also strengthened my belief that Kirana retailers form a community of our own. We share a bond that transcends geographic boundaries, and this book is proof of that unity. It has allowed me to connect with my peers in different cities, learn about their challenges, and admire their innovative approaches to the business.

I would like to express my gratitude for the opportunity to contribute to this book and for the valuable insights it offers. This book speaks to the heart of Kirana retail, providing a glimpse into the lives of those who dedicate themselves to this profession. It celebrates our resilience, adaptability, and our unwavering commitment to our communities. To my fellow Kirana retailers and everyone who has been part of this journey, thank you. Your stories have made this book a true reflection of our lives, and I am proud to be part of this shared narrative that highlights the heart and soul of Kirana retail in India.

--==--

Preface

In the winding streets and quiet corners of India, a unique and enduring aspect of the retail landscape thrives – the Kirana stores. Known by various names such as 'Kirana Retailers,' 'Mom & Pop Stores,' 'Bricks & Mortar Shops,' 'Grocers,' 'Kiranawalas,' or 'Pansaris,' these small neighbourhood shops are an essential part of everyday life.

These modest stores represent more than just places of business. They are the guardians of tradition, champions of sustainability, and centres of community.

Kirana stores come in many forms. From long-established family-run shops to specialised outlets catering to specific needs, they showcase remarkable diversity. Many have successfully combined traditional practices with modern business models, offering online shopping and adopting hybrid approaches that link the past with the future.

Far from being mere points of commerce, Kirana stores are the heart of their communities. They serve as spaces for social interaction and are instrumental in creating strong community bonds.

At the core of their success is sound financial management. Careful budgeting and planning are crucial, guiding these businesses through the challenges of retail. In addition, many Kirana stores have embraced technology, fintech solutions, and community-driven initiatives to improve their operations.

Kirana retailers are not simply providers of goods but also active participants in their communities. Their role extends beyond commerce, embodying social responsibility, fostering community engagement, and supporting local initiatives.

Though their commitment to sustainability is often understated, it is an integral part of their daily operations. These stores often stock locally sourced products, minimise plastic usage, and advocate for eco-friendly alternatives, reflecting their dedication to environmental responsibility.

More than just retail outlets, Kirana stores are hubs of human connection. Regular customers are greeted by familiar faces, and personal relationships are formed over time. Kirana store owners often extend a helping hand in times of need, standing as symbols of support and social cohesion in a world that is increasingly digital and isolated.

Recognising their significance, many businesses are now forming partnerships with Kirana stores to enhance their growth. Companies such as Kiranaking, Metro Cash & Carry, Jiomart, Grofers, Amazon, and Flipkart are offering various forms of assistance, including supply chain solutions, access to e-commerce platforms, and last-mile delivery services. These collaborations also provide reverse logistics, streamlining product returns and operations.

Looking towards the future, the prospects for Kirana retail are promising. These stores, renowned for their adaptability, are set to embrace further technological advancements, place greater emphasis on sustainability, diversify their offerings, and form collaborations with tech startups and e-commerce platforms. Traditional distributors and wholesalers will continue to play a crucial role, embracing digital transformation and supporting local sourcing.

This book provides a comprehensive exploration of Kirana stores, which are far more than places to shop. They represent pillars of tradition, sustainability, and community in India, leaving a lasting influence on society.

Kirana retailers are the unsung heroes of social cohesion and small business success. Their contributions extend well beyond the doors of their modest stores, proving that even the smallest of businesses can have a profound impact on society.

As the Hindi saying goes, **Kirana retailers are the backbone of the country** – a testament to their enduring and invaluable contribution to India's retail landscape

Acknowledgements

In my journey to explore the complexities of Kirana retail, I have had the privilege of standing at the intersection of tradition and innovation, bridging the gap between the old and the new, and celebrating the core of Indian retail. This journey would not have been possible without the generous support of individuals and businesses who welcomed me with open arms and shared their valuable insights, experiences, and dreams.

On behalf of everyone involved, I would like to express my sincere gratitude to all the Kirana retailers from Jaipur, Delhi, Mumbai, Hyderabad, Chennai, Bangalore, Ahmedabad, Indore, and beyond, who dedicated their time and provided the foundation for this exploration of Kirana retail. Their contributions have been crucial in shaping the story that follows.

I would like to extend my heartfelt thanks to **Mr. Anup K Kumar, Founder & CEO of Kirana King**, and my esteemed colleague, for their exceptional contributions to the upliftment of Kirana retailers. Mr. Kumar has truly made a remarkable impact by transforming the Kirana landscape, particularly in Jaipur. His visionary leadership and unwavering commitment to supporting local businesses have resulted in the uplifting of 250 stores across the city, empowering these retailers to thrive in a competitive world.

Through substantial investments and a dedication to excellence, Mr. Kumar has not only enhanced the infrastructure and operations of these stores but has also positioned them as the stores of choice for the community. His efforts have created lasting value, improving the livelihoods of Kirana owners and providing consumers with a superior shopping experience.

This remarkable journey reflects his passion for innovation and his dedication to the Kirana sector, ensuring that these small businesses are equipped to succeed in an ever-changing market. Thank you, Mr. Kumar, for your visionary work and for being a true champion of the Kirana retailer community.

I would like to start by expressing my deepest appreciation to **Mr. Ajay Gupta, Managing Director of Kamtech in Jaipur**. His openness and insightful perspectives on Kirana retail have been instrumental in understanding the challenges and opportunities faced by small neighbourhood stores across India. His leadership in the industry has been a guiding light throughout this journey.

Mr. Akshay Vijay, the owner of R R Departmental Store in Model Town, Jaipur, has been an invaluable source of firsthand knowledge. His willingness to share the daily challenges and triumphs of a local store owner has provided a real-world perspective central to understanding the pulse of Kirana retail.

Kalpataru Departmental Store in Jagatpura, Jaipur, led by Mr. Pawan Sharma, has been another cornerstone in this exploration. His dedication to retail, commitment to community engagement, and insights into the role of Kirana stores as social hubs have greatly enriched this understanding.

In Patel Marg, **Mansarovar, Jaipur, Mr. Pawan of Mangal Traders** has generously shared his expertise on the financial intricacies and cash flow management essential for running a Kirana store. His insights into channel financing have been invaluable.

The contributions of these distinguished Kirana retailers reflect the dedication and passion of the entire Kirana retail community. Their experiences represent the challenges, aspirations, and dreams of many others who form the backbone of India's retail sector.

As I goes with this journey, I realized that the voices of Kirana retailers went beyond geographical borders. The insights shared in Jaipur were echoed in the busy lanes of Delhi, the vibrant streets of Mumbai, the rich cultural neighbourhoods of Hyderabad, the diverse markets of Chennai, the tech-savvy areas of Bangalore, the entrepreneurial spirit of Ahmedabad, and the dynamic trade hubs of Indore. Through the collective wisdom of Kirana retailers from these various regions, a comprehensive understanding of India's retail landscape emerged.

The voices of Kirana retailers have not only shaped this exploration but have also deepened my appreciation for their resilience and adaptability. Their stories highlight the challenges they face in an ever-changing market, their commitment to sustainability, their social impact, and their readiness to embrace technology and innovation to succeed in the digital age.

I extend my sincere gratitude to all the Kirana retailers who participated in this journey, whether by sharing their experiences, providing insights, or offering suggestions. This project would not have been possible without their support, and their voices have brought authenticity and depth to the narrative that follows.

A **heartfelt thanks to over 1000 Kirana retailers who shared their insights during my research across cities in 2013-14, including Chennai, Bangalore, Hyderabad, Ahmedabad, Mumbai, Indore, Lucknow, Kolkata, Delhi,**

Chandigarh, Jammu, and Rohtak. I spent 7 months engaging with these dedicated individuals, gaining invaluable perspectives on Kirana retail. Your contributions were crucial in shaping this book, and I am deeply grateful for your participation and support.

--==--

Prologue

The prologue takes us deep into the world of Kirana retail, an often-underestimated yet essential pillar of India's retail ecosystem. These small neighborhood stores, frequently overshadowed by the rise of modern retail chains, represent more than just businesses—they embody resilience, community spirit, and an unwavering connection with the people they serve. In this journey, I delve into the challenges and triumphs faced by Kirana retailers, shedding light on their adaptability and commitment to their communities in a rapidly evolving retail environment.

The Heart of Kirana Retail

Kirana retail is more than a transactional business—it is an integral part of the social fabric of India. These stores are not just points of sale but hubs that foster community interactions and uphold traditional values. As custodians of local culture, they sponsor events, support charitable causes, and provide a sense of belonging that is often missing in today's fast-paced world. They are the lifeblood of neighborhoods, making them indispensable to the social cohesion that holds these communities together.

Facing the Challenges of Modern Retail

The Kirana store faces a multitude of challenges. The rise of large retail chains and the dominance of e-commerce platforms are squeezing these small retailers from all sides. Declining sales, shifting consumer behaviors, and the need for technological adaptation are creating immense pressure on these neighborhood stores. However, it is in the face of these challenges that the true strength of Kirana retailers shines. Their resilience and ability to adapt—whether through digital integration or changing their business models—are key to their survival.

A Collective Story of Resilience

The stories I've gathered from across India show that Kirana retailers share a collective resilience that transcends regional boundaries. Whether it's in the bustling streets of Mumbai or the quiet corners of rural India, these retailers are united by a common thread: the drive to serve their communities, to adapt, and to thrive despite the challenges. This book is a tribute to that spirit of resilience and the remarkable ability of Kirana retailers to evolve while staying true to their roots.

Insights for Transformation

To truly understand the future of Kirana retail, we must look at how these retailers are embracing change. Financial management, sustainability, and digital transformation are the cornerstones of their growth. This book highlights how Kirana retailers are adopting fintech solutions, integrating technology into their operations, and embracing sustainable practices that meet the changing needs of their customers. These insights are not just theoretical—they are practical, actionable steps that can help these retailers thrive in the face of modern challenges.

A Call to Action

As you turn these pages, I invite you to explore the world of Kirana retail in all its complexity. These retailers are not just running businesses; they are holding together the social and economic fabric of India. This book is a testament to their dedication, their ability to transform, and their unwavering commitment to the communities they serve. Through their stories, we can see the true heart of Indian retail, and understand the crucial role that Kirana stores will continue to play in the future.

--==--

ONE

Market Overview and Kirana Retailer's Role

The retail ecosystem is witnessing significant development worldwide. The size of the Indian retail market, which was around **$425 billion in 2010, is now estimated to be $800 billion as of 2022, with a Compound Annual Growth Rate (CAGR) of 6.5% over a 10-year period. Projections for the next 5-10 years suggest a 10% annual growth,** with market sources predicting it will reach $1.3 trillion by 2025-26 and beyond. The past five years, in particular, have seen a surge driven by a dramatic shift in consumer behavior, startup enthusiasm, the use of technology, significant investments that have fostered startups, created unicorns, and introduced disruptions. One such disruption is the rise of

Quick Commerce (Q-commerce), a rapidly growing segment of retail that is redefining convenience by offering hyper-local deliveries within minutes. This new model has had a significant impact on grocery retail, as platforms like Dunzo, Blinkit, and Zepto cater to the fast-paced, on-demand needs of urban consumers.

As a retail professional, my admiration for Indian retail, especially grocery (Kirana) retail, began with my first interaction with Sachin Bansal of Flipkart in 2012. This experience revealed the immense size and potential of Indian retail and marked the beginning of my journey into the retail sector. I soon became a learning professional, visiting Kirana shops and trying to understand the ecosystem that sustained them.

I was responsible for backward integration in the supply chain, focusing on developing products and transforming the trade of staples from 'loose' items to attractively packaged and hygienically sealed products for high-end consumers. Initially, most staple goods were traded in bulk or loose formats, with traders selling 25kg and 50kg packs to retailers, who then sold them in loose packaging using paper or cloth bags. Although my initial role had limited interaction with front-end sales, I realized that to gain innovative ideas and stay informed about market developments, I needed to be in the field—understanding market sentiments, new entrants in the grocery sector, the competitive landscape, and more. I began visiting people, places, and product manufacturing units, gaining a comprehensive view of the market and identifying key stakeholders.

I graduated in 1998 and joined a Delhi-based export house as an account clerk. They were involved in the manufacturing and export of menthol and were one of the largest importers of pulses. Later, I was tasked with selling pulses in 1kg pouches as an area salesman, covering South Delhi. It was during this role that I first encountered Kirana retailers and recognized their vital role in the retail ecosystem. They served as brand ambassadors, offering retail space for a wide range of products and promoting them to their local customers, helping FMCG companies establish their products as brands. At that time, the term 'Marka'—an anglicized version of 'brand'—was commonly used in the ecosystem.

This is where the role of retailers begins. Let's examine how they fulfill their roles and the daily sacrifices they make. Can you imagine the share of Kirana retail in India, say up to 2010?

Market Share of General Trade, Modern Trade & E-commerce:

Segmentation in the market began after 2006 with the launch of Future Group and various hypermarkets, which led to better visibility and an enhanced consumer experience. FMCG companies began customizing trade terms and strategies for General Trade, Modern Trade, and E-commerce.

Contribution of General Trade:

Currently, more than 12-14 million retailers contribute to 85% of total retail, yet they remain largely unorganised. While urban areas have a higher consumption size, rural markets are experiencing significant growth. The General Trade market is expanding rapidly in rural areas, with both FMCG companies and retailers having various supply chain options. Greater focus is needed to organise this sector and bring it into the mainstream. General retailers are gradually changing their shop appearances to align with new developments, though the pace is slow.

Contribution of Modern Trade:

Until **2010, 99% of General Retail was in the hands of stand-alone Kirana stores**, although market reports suggest it was 95% at that time. It's still unclear who made up the remaining **5% of organised retail**. Notable players like Dmart, Subiksha, 6Ten, Big Bazaar, Reliance Fresh, More, Vishal Mega Mart, Spencers, Walmart, LOTs, and Metro C&C had a limited presence in terms of revenue, coverage, and penetration until 2010. However, their impact on Kirana stores cannot be ignored, especially in the grocery segment. Significant changes in the market began from 2012 onwards.

D-mart opened its first store in Powai, Maharashtra, in 2002, and by 2022, it operated 294 stores in 11+ cities. Its rapid expansion has helped it become one of India's leading retail chains. D-mart, along with other corporates like Localmart in Gujarat, has affected Kirana retailers and general stores. Stand-alone supermarkets in each city now contribute up to 10% of their respective retail markets.

In the south, Ratnadeep has over 100 stores.

These modern trade formats contribute 10-15% to the total retail segment. However, in the grocery segment, their share is approximately 5% of the total retail market, estimated to be around $800 billion. This represents a small portion of the larger pie, with 85% still in the hands of unorganised retailers. The rise of Q-commerce, however, is challenging this dominance, particularly in urban areas, with many consumers opting for faster, on-demand deliveries rather than traditional shopping methods.

A market survey by https://www.statista.com

Value of the retail market in India from 2018 to 2020, with estimates until 2026
(in billion U.S. dollars)

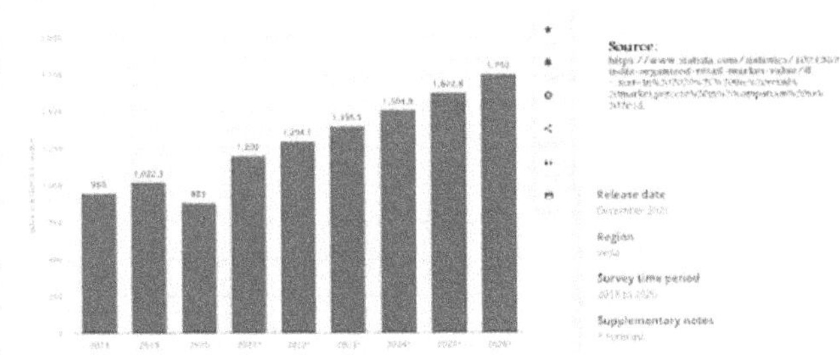

Enter Caption

The market began introducing new terminology to FMCG (Fast-Moving Consumer Goods) companies, and soon they realized that modern trade in the form of chain stores was the future of grocery retail in India. Consequently, they began developing different product assortments, pricing, and promotional strategies for modern trade and beyond.

Contribution of E-Commerce Trade

B2C E-Commerce - Consumer-focused, with new catchy terms like Social Commerce, Hyperlocal, Omnichannel, and more, contributing a total of $84 billion to retail.

Simultaneously, e-commerce, with a consumer-centric approach, is rapidly expanding. Marketplaces like Amazon and Flipkart have become platforms where brands sell products across various categories, including groceries. On the other side, B2C grocery platforms such as **JioMart, Grofers, DealShare, Citymall, and Milkbasket are among the startups adopting a direct-to-consumer (D2C) approach.**

Don't be confused by their names, which include terms like convenience stores, priority, hyperlocal, omnichannel commerce, social commerce, and Q-commerce. The goal is clear: how to sell products directly to consumers.

Quick-commerce - a new term in the world of e-commerce. Significant developments are happening in the grocery market. Now, it's time for Q-commerce players like **Zepto, Blinkit (formerly Grofers), Swiggy's Instamart**, and many more to establish a region-specific presence. Zepto, Blinkit, and Instamart are national players with a presence in major cities. They provide rapid delivery services, offering consumers the ability to receive their orders within 10-15 minutes.

From a data perspective, it's worth noting that e-commerce has not yet reached a size of over $100 billion.

In the name of disruptions, we can observe these developments. I am not criticizing their beginnings and existence. It's positive that the retail sector is evolving and expanding day by day. However, one aspect we must consider is the extent of change needed to disrupt the existing ecosystem. We must acknowledge that:

India has had retail for centuries, but the key lies in modernizing it by empowering the existing setup, business practices, and connecting them with consumers. In today's evolving customer landscape, there's a need for changes in the working and operations of unorganized or traditional store owners. Kiranas, or traditional store owners, play a crucial role in the Indian consumption ecosystem. They have been closely connected to their customers, understanding their needs and adjusting merchandise in line with seasonal and festive requirements. Even today, if we visit our local Kirana store, they know the pulses we buy and the brands we prefer.

Despite this, we are actively disrupting them through modern trade, e-commerce, social commerce, and Q-commerce. Perhaps, in the near future, we might witness another form of commerce, maybe based on meta. I refer to these as adversaries of Kiranawalas. They are the culprits aiming to engulf them without remorse.

Still, 85% of retail is driven by small retailers, known as Mom & Pop stores or Kiranawalas, and their contribution to GDP is outstanding, accounting for up to 10-11%. They also generate around 8% of the country's employment.

As per market data, retail is expected to reach a size of $1.2 trillion soon. There will be opportunities for all stakeholders, but Kirana retailers might have the least share. Based on my survey in the Jaipur market, one D-mart store alone can diminish the business of nearby Kirana stores by 30-40%. When news circulates that D-mart is opening a store in a particular locality, you can see the concern in retailers' eyes and the anxiety about losing business. They fear D-mart because it poses a significant threat to their businesses. JioMart, another major player, is also on the verge of affecting Kiranawalas, although it appears friendly and portrays itself as a B2B player.

The same goes for Q-commerce players offering 10-15-minute deliveries to end consumers, as they are taking a substantial share of business from Kiranawalas. End consumers now turn to Kirana stores primarily for impulsive or just-in-time purchases, which Q-commerce players are now fulfilling.

It's a fact that these developments in e-commerce and large offline retail chains are impacting Kirana retailers, and the magnitude of such activities is increasing day by day. I conducted a soft survey on several A and B class outlets in Jaipur, and I've known most of these retailers for a long time. Previously, they generated monthly revenues of 10-15 lakh. However, the situation has changed. Competition from B2C and big box retailers has become more intense than ever, causing retailers to suffer substantial losses. They now generate 5-7 lakh per month, and customer footfall is decreasing daily, with almost a 50% reduction in business over the past two years. A significant transformation in the name of disruption is underway.

Courage of retailers: I congratulate all store owners for standing strong against tough competition. Their personalized relationships with consumers are the reason they have survived. Otherwise, they would have closed their stores long ago. In the face of market forces, an individual can't do much or oppose changes. Change is inevitable, and everyone must adapt.

--==--

TWO

INTRODUCTION TO KIRANA RETAILERS

Kirana retailers play a crucial role in India's retail landscape, serving as pillars of resilience and adaptability. These small, family-run businesses are known by many names, such as Kiranawala, Pansari, corner shop, Mom & Pop store, and countless regional terms. Each name reflects the rich linguistic diversity of India, showcasing how deeply embedded these retailers are in the country's cultural fabric. Despite their small size, Kirana stores make up a significant portion of India's retail sector, representing the true spirit of grassroots commerce.

Kirana stores are found at the heart of local communities, often positioned on street corners or tucked away in neighbourhoods. They are more than just places to buy daily essentials; they are the lifeblood of the community. These stores create a sense of familiarity and trust, offering a personalised shopping experience that larger retail chains cannot replicate. Whether it is a quick chat with the shopkeeper or the comfort of knowing the store has exactly what you need, Kirana retailers form an integral part of everyday life.

What makes these stores particularly unique is their ability to adapt to the changing needs of the community. Despite facing increasing competition from modern retail outlets and e-commerce platforms, Kirana stores continue to thrive by building strong customer relationships and providing exceptional service. Many Kirana owners have embraced new technologies, improving inventory management and customer engagement, while still retaining the traditional values that make them so beloved.

Kirana retailers are not just business owners; they are trusted community members who understand the pulse of the neighbourhood. They create deep-rooted connections with customers, offer valuable local products, and contribute to the economy in ways that extend far beyond simple transactions. Their significance cannot be overstated, as they shape daily life, promote local commerce, and help sustain communities across India.

The Charm of Kirana Retail

There is a certain charm in Kirana retail—a charm that hides the complexities beneath its surface. These shops, often small, with modest spaces of around 120 to 200 square feet, are the epitome of simplicity. However, behind this simplicity lies a sophisticated ballet of commerce, where the shopkeeper, through a seamless blend of skill and intuition, navigates the constantly shifting dynamics of supply, demand, and consumer preferences. The Kirana retailer is a multifaceted entrepreneur, simultaneously managing inventory, finances, customer relations, and community engagement.

A Range of Sizes and Success Narratives

Walk into any neighbourhood and you'll encounter these humble shops, seamlessly integrated into the everyday rhythm of life. **Around 60% of Kirana stores are housed in modest spaces of 120 to 200 square feet, another 30% stretch to 300-500 square feet, while the remaining 10% occupy larger premises. But here's the truth—size is**n't the key measure of success in this business.

Size Deception

In the world of Kirana retail, bigger doesn't always mean better. Some small stores, confined to just 300 square feet, generate monthly revenues exceeding ₹20 lakhs, while others with more extensive spaces struggle to **cross the ₹ 5-10 lakh threshold**. Across India, approximately 12 million Kirana stores contribute a significant ₹600 billion to the economy, demonstrating that size isn't always the determinant of success.

Behind the Numbers

Delving deeper into the workings of these stores, we see the true story unfold. Smaller shops, often with a space of under 120 square feet, stock anywhere between **300 to 500 SKUs, primarily focusing on daily essentials like milk, rice, and flour. Their daily sales range from ₹5,000 to ₹7,500, translating into a monthly turnover of ₹ 1.5-2.25 lakh, with tight margins of 12-15%. In reality, the owners make a meagre ₹18,000- ₹25,000 a month, highlighting the immense eff**ort and persistence it takes to sustain these businesses with limited sales and razor-thin profits.

The 80/20 Rule in Kirana Retail

The 80/20 rule holds true even in Kirana retail. A select group of retailers, classified into A, B, and C categories, controls 80% of the business in their areas. The remaining 20% is divided among smaller, D, E, and other categories of retailers.

A Life of Dedication

Is starting a Kirana business as easy as it seems? The truth is, it's not. While the concept might appear simple, the reality is far more demanding. These shops open early, around 6 AM, and often stay open until 8-10 PM. For Kirana shopkeepers, their business is their life—requiring complete dedication, often at the expense of their personal time and social life.

A Testament to Indomitable Spirit

In the world of Kirana retail, resilience is more than a quality—it's a way of life. It's a testament to the spirit of these entrepreneurs who, with grace and perseverance, navigate the complexities of commerce and adapt to ever-changing market dynamics. As India's retail sector continues to evolve, the Kirana store remains a pillar of local commerce, preserving the essence of community even as it embraces change.

धूप में बैठना अब मेरे बस की बात नहीं, किराना का दुकानदार हूँ,
रोज़ाना काम करने का मै हकदार हूँ।

Perfect quote for Kirana retailers

Kirana stores, the ever-present corner shops in every neighbourhood of India, are not just places to buy groceries; they are the very heart of communities. These small, family-operated businesses offer essential items, personalised service, and an unmatched sense of connection that large supermarkets or e-commerce platforms simply cannot provide.

From their humble beginnings as grocery stores to their modern-day embrace of technology, Kirana stores have played a pivotal role in shaping India's retail landscape. They stand as a symbol of the resilience and adaptability of Indian businesses, proving that even in the face of change, the corner store remains a cherished part of Indian life.

The Corner Store: A Pillar of Indian Retail

Picture a small, busy shop tucked away in the heart of a neighbourhood, filled with the delightful aroma of fresh spices and the sounds of familiar voices. This is the essence of the Kirana store, the lifeblood of Indian retail.

Local Presence and Accessibility: Apna Dukan, Apna Saaman

Kirana stores, much like a trusted companion, are always within reach. Whether situated in the hustle of a bustling city or the peacefulness of a village, they are the first place people turn to for their daily needs.

Diverse Product Range: Aapki Pasand, Hamaari Khaas

From the essential rice and lentils that form the backbone of Indian cooking, to fresh vegetables from local farms, and everyday household items, Kirana stores are a treasure trove of necessities.

Personalized Service: Dil Se Dua, Naam Se Pukar

Walking into a Kirana store feels like being enveloped in a warm embrace. There is a familiarity in the air. The shopkeepers, often called "Bhaiyya" or "Aunty," greet their customers with a smile, knowing their preferences and understanding their needs.

Credit Facilities: Aapke Saath, Hum Bhi Saath

Kirana stores go beyond being mere retail outlets; they are lifelines for many. Offering credit to regular customers, these stores show trust and understanding, ensuring that essential items are never out of reach.

Local Sourcing and Supply Chain: Gaon Se Plate Tak

Kirana stores are deeply woven into the fabric of the local economy, connecting producers and consumers. They source products from a network of local suppliers, including farmers, artisans, and wholesalers, strengthening the economic ties within their communities.

Community Integration: Aapka Adda, Humara Sarafa

These stores are not just about buying goods—they are the pillars of community life. Kirana shops act as informal gathering spaces where neighbours come together to chat, share news, and foster a sense of belonging.

--==--

THREE

Significance of Kirana Stores in India Jug Jug Jiye, Kirana

Kirana stores are an indispensable part of India's retail landscape, contributing significantly to both the economy and the social fabric of the nation. These small, local businesses serve as vital touchstones within communities, offering much more than just goods for sale—they are symbols of accessibility, trust, and resilience.

Accessibility and Convenience: "Jab Bhi Zaroorat, Tab Bhi Haazir"

Kirana stores are ubiquitous, always within easy reach. Whether nestled in a busy urban corner or in more remote rural areas, they provide unparalleled convenience to customers, offering essential products whenever needed. This accessibility is particularly crucial for those with limited mobility or for individuals living in areas where larger retail outlets or e-commerce services may not be as readily available. In these areas, Kirana stores bridge a critical gap, ensuring that no one is left wanting for everyday necessities.

Economic Contribution: "Desh Ka Rozgar, Kirana Ka Sahara"

Beyond their role in serving the community, Kirana stores are also powerful economic engines. They provide employment opportunities not only to shopkeepers but also to delivery personnel, local suppliers, and countless others within their supply chains. Kirana stores play a vital role in generating local tax revenue, further contributing to the economic health of the regions in which they operate. In fact, the sheer scale of the Kirana sector provides jobs to millions, making it an essential contributor to India's workforce.

Personalisation and Trust: "Bhaiyya Ji Ka Haath, Sahi Hai Baat"

One of the defining features of Kirana stores is the personalised service they offer. Unlike large retail chains, where interactions may often feel impersonal, Kirana store owners develop close relationships with their customers. These bonds of trust and familiarity foster a sense of loyalty that is hard to replicate. A simple conversation with the shopkeeper, who knows your preferences, creates an invaluable sense of security and reliability that customers have come to cherish.

Flexibility and Credit Facilities: "Jab Paisa Nahin Ho, Tab Bhi Saath"

Kirana stores often act as a financial lifeline for individuals facing temporary cash constraints. With their practice of extending credit facilities, these stores ensure that essential goods remain within reach, even for those unable to pay upfront. This practice, built on mutual trust and understanding, is especially important in communities where access to formal credit systems may be limited. The Kirana store, in this sense, is not just a place of commerce but a crucial safety net for many households.

Community Centres: "Apna Adda, Humara Sarafa"

Kirana stores also serve as vital community centres, where social interaction and local culture thrive. These shops are often gathering points where people exchange news, share stories, and strengthen bonds. They are more than just transactional spaces; they are the heartbeat of local social life, fostering a sense of belonging and camaraderie. In many ways, these stores help preserve and propagate local traditions, acting as a hub for cultural exchange and mutual support within communities.

Balancing the Retail Landscape: "Supermarket Aur Kirana, Ek Saath"

Despite the growing presence of large retail chains and e-commerce platforms, Kirana stores continue to coexist harmoniously within the broader retail landscape. Rather than being replaced or overshadowed, they complement the larger retail sector by offering a more personalised, community-focused alternative to the impersonal shopping experiences that supermarkets or online platforms may provide. This balance allows consumers to enjoy the best of both worlds: the convenience and variety of larger outlets combined with the personal touch and reliability of their local Kirana shop.

In conclusion, Kirana stores are much more than just shops—they are cornerstones of India's economy and community life. Their enduring presence underscores the importance of accessibility, trust, and social cohesion in our rapidly changing world. Whether through their economic contributions, personalised service, or the social bonds they create, Kirana stores will continue to play an essential role in shaping India's retail landscape for years to come.

Data on Kirana Stores in India

In the heart of every Indian neighbourhood lies an unassuming yet indispensable establishment – the Kirana store. These ubiquitous corner shops, often affectionately known as "mom-and-pop" stores, are not merely retail outlets; they are the lifeblood of communities, weaving a tapestry of accessibility, personalized service, and social connection that has stood the test of time.

Kirana stores account for over 90% of India's vast \$540 billion retail market, a testament to their pervasive presence and deep-rooted connection with consumers. Their sheer number, estimated at over 12-14 million, forms one of the world's largest retail networks.

Far from being relics of the past, Kirana stores have embraced technology, with a growing number adopting mobile apps and point-of-sale (POS) systems to streamline operations and enhance the customer experience. This digital transformation reflects their resilience and adaptability in an ever-evolving retail landscape.

Beyond their retail function, Kirana stores serve as community hubs, fostering a sense of belonging and connection. They are the go-to places for exchanging news, sharing stories, and forging bonds that strengthen the social fabric of neighbourhoods.

Their economic impact is equally profound. Kirana stores are not just places to buy groceries; they are generators of employment, supporting local suppliers and distributors, and offering credit facilities to patrons in need. They are the backbone of local economies, contributing significantly to India's overall retail ecosystem.

The personalized service offered by Kirana store owners is a hallmark of their success. They know their customers' preferences, anticipate their needs, and build relationships that extend beyond mere transactions. This personal touch fosters trust and loyalty, setting them apart from larger retail chains.

In an era of e-commerce and supermarket dominance, Kirana stores have not only survived but thrived. They have adapted to changing consumer preferences, embraced technology, and retained their core identity – the friendly neighbourhood store that knows its customers and serves as a pillar of the community.

Kirana stores are more than just retail establishments; they are embodiments of India's retail landscape, embodying accessibility, personalized service, and community. Their importance extends to economic, social, and cultural dimensions, making them an indispensable institution in the country. Their ability to evolve and endure in changing times reflects their adaptability to shifting consumer needs, securing their place as a cherished part of Indian life.

--==--

FOUR

Kirana Retail Ecosystem

The Indian Kirana retailer ecosystem is a vibrant mosaic of vitality, weaving together a network of small, local grocery stores that play a pivotal role in the nation's retail landscape. These Kirana stores, affectionately known as "mom-and-pop" shops, are intricately entwined in the daily lives of countless Indians. Their hallmark lies in accessibility, serving as repositories of a diverse array of goods, ranging from essential groceries to household necessities and beyond.

However, what truly distinguishes Kirana stores is their embodiment of personalized service. Here, customer relationships transcend mere transactions, forming enduring bonds built on the foundation of trust. Furthermore, Kirana stores showcase an exceptional ability to adapt and pivot, gracefully navigating the evolving currents of consumer preferences and market dynamics. In this process, they have embraced technology and modern retail practices.

Yet, the Kirana store is more than a mere emporium of goods; it is a community epicenter where people converge, creating social connections and nurturing relationships. Remarkably, these establishments contribute significantly to localized economic growth by sourcing their wares from nearby wholesalers and suppliers, thereby supporting the livelihoods of many.

This vibrant ecosystem coexists harmoniously with large supermarket chains and the unstoppable wave of e-commerce platforms, offering a diverse and intricately textured retail landscape in India. Essentially, the Kirana store is not just a retailer; it is a living thread woven into the intricate tapestry of the nation's social and economic fabric.

Types of Kirana Stores in India

Kirana stores in India come in various forms, each serving distinct purposes within the retail landscape. Understanding these types is crucial for appreciating the diversity within Kirana retail. Here are some of the most prevalent types of Kirana stores:

1. **Traditional Kirana Stores :** Traditional Kirana stores are the bedrock of the Indian retail industry, typically stocking a diverse range of everyday items, from groceries and toiletries to household necessities. These stores are renowned for their personalized service and unparalleled convenience.

2. **Provision Stores :** Provision stores are a specialized type of Kirana store that focuses on stocking basic food items such as grains, lentils, rice, and other staples. These stores cater primarily to customers who are looking for essential food items and cooking ingredients.

3. **Specialty Kirana Stores**: Some Kirana stores specialize in specific product categories, such as sweets, spices, or snacks. These specialty stores offer a unique and carefully curated selection of items designed to meet the specific preferences of their customers.

4. **Organic Kirana Stores**: In response to the growing interest in organic and health-conscious products, some Kirana stores have been transformed into organic outlets. These stores offer organic produce, natural foods, and environmentally friendly products. Examples include Morarka's Down to Earth stores, which showcase their organic product range, and 24 Mantra stores.

5. **Mini Supermarkets**: Mini supermarkets, also known as walk-through stores, are a larger version of the traditional Kirana store. They often stock a wider variety of products, including fresh produce, dairy, and frozen foods. Mini supermarkets aim to provide a supermarket-like shopping experience while retaining the core essence of a Kirana store. Jaipur city has more than 150 stores in this category.

6. **Retail Chains**: A retail chain is a network of interconnected stores or outlets that are owned and operated by the same company. These stores are often located in different locations and share a common brand, management, and supply chain. Retail chains in the grocery industry aim to provide a consistent shopping experience, standardized product offerings, and efficient distribution of goods. Examples include Dmart, Reliance Fresh, Spencers, Ratanadeep, Nilgris, Ipertmart in Rajasthan, National Super Mart in Jaipur, Localmarts in Gujarat and Maharashtra, Bigmart in Kolkata, etc. Other examples include Sampat Namkeen

in Jaipur, Narayan ji Gajjak, 11 No in Khari Baoli, Delhi, and many more.

7. **Urban Kirana Stores:** Urban Kirana stores are commonly found in cities and densely populated urban areas. They cater to the fast-paced urban lifestyle by offering convenience foods, ready-to-eat meals, and a diverse range of snacks.

Section 2: Ownership Structures

Ownership structures within the Kirana store ecosystem exhibit remarkable diversity, with family-owned businesses, partnerships, and franchises being common models. Comprehending these ownership structures is essential for grasping the richness of the Kirana landscape.

Family-Owned Kirana Stores: The majority of Kirana stores in India are family-owned and operated. These businesses are often handed down through generations, with active family involvement in day-to-day operations.

Partnerships and Co-Ownership: Some Kirana stores are jointly-owned by multiple individuals, frequently friends or extended family members. In such arrangements, each partner may contribute to the business through capital investment or labour.

Franchised Kirana Stores: In recent years, the franchise model has gained traction among Kirana stores. Franchised Kirana stores operate under the branding and support of larger retail chains. This approach offers standardised processes and access to a broader product range.

Cooperative Societies: In certain regions, cooperative societies of Kirana store owners have emerged. These cooperatives enable small store owners to collectively purchase inventory, negotiate with suppliers, and realise the benefits of economies of scale.

Section 3: Business Models

Business models within the Kirana store ecosystem have undergone significant evolution to adapt to changing consumer preferences and market dynamics. Diverse models cater to a wide array of customer segments and preferences. Here are some common Kirana store business models:

Traditional Kirana Model: The traditional Kirana store model focuses on providing a wide variety of everyday products with a personalised touch. Owners often rely on robust customer relationships to drive business.

Online and App-Based Kirana Model: With the proliferation of smartphones, many Kirana stores have embraced technology. They offer online ordering and delivery through mobile apps, allowing customers to shop conveniently from the comfort of their homes.

Hybrid Model: Some Kirana stores have adopted a hybrid model, combining traditional in-store shopping with online ordering and delivery services. This approach offers flexibility to customers, catering to both online and offline shopping preferences.

Mini Supermarket Model: Mini supermarkets or walkthrough stores operate on a larger scale and often carry a broader variety of products. They aim to provide a more extensive shopping experience while retaining the convenience and familiarity of a Kirana store.

Specialty Store Model: Specialty Kirana stores focus on niche product categories, such as organic foods, gourmet items, or regional specialties. These stores cater to specific customer interests, offering a unique shopping experience.

Understanding the diversity of business models within the Kirana ecosystem sheds light on the adaptability and innovation of these small retailers. They continue to evolve and cater to a wide range of customer needs, contributing significantly to India's retail sector.

In this Chapter, we have explored the various types of Kirana stores, ownership structures, and business models that together comprise the dynamic Kirana store ecosystem in India. These distinctions underscore the adaptability and resilience of Kirana stores as they persist in serving the diverse needs of Indian consumers

--==--

FIVE

Challenges and Opportunities

The Indian Kirana retail ecosystem, marked by both challenges and opportunities, is being navigated by small store owners with resilience and adaptability. The complexities of their business journey are highlighted by increasing competition from large retail chains and e-commerce platforms, alongside the necessity for modernization and technological integration. However, efforts are being made to counter these obstacles through innovation, such as broadening product offerings, diversifying services, and adopting technology to enhance efficiency and customer experience.

Regulatory policies and government initiatives are also shaping this sector, impacting the operation and growth of Kirana stores. Insights into these aspects demonstrate how small businesses can sustain themselves amidst the changing retail landscape in India. This dynamic landscape underscores the balance between traditional practices and modern retail approaches.

The Indian retail industry stands apart from its organized counterparts in developed countries. While modern retail formats dominate in the West, Indian retail continues to be led by Kirana stores—family-run businesses operating traditionally. The unorganized nature of these stores presents unique challenges, especially in a semi-modern India.

The economic rise, seen in the growing middle-class population in Tier 1 to Tier 3 cities, has altered shopping habits. With increased disposable incomes, consumers now prefer convenience and modern shopping experiences. This has pressured Kirana owners to adapt to meet evolving demands. Adopting innovative strategies, blending traditional methods with modern practices, has become essential.

Organized retail, exemplified by players like Reliance Fresh, Big Bazaar, and DMart, has expanded significantly, often taking up enormous retail spaces in cities. Similarly, e-commerce giants such as Amazon and Walmart leverage data and technology to boost transaction values. Yet, challenges remain for both sectors in achieving profitability. Despite the rise of organized retail and e-commerce, Kirana stores are expected to endure in India for decades.

Experts like **Metro Cash & Carry India's MD, Arvind Mediratta, have highlighted the importance of Kirana stores in the economy.** He emphasizes collaboration between large retailers and Kiranas to modernize operations without threatening their existence. Moreover, calls for increased margins by FMCG companies aim to ensure sustainable profits for Kirana owners.

Insights derived from extensive surveys and interviews reveal that the upcoming years hold promise for grocery retail, with IT solutions like POS systems, auto-replenishment, and banking services being introduced to aid Kirana stores. A shift in consumer behaviour toward quality over branding, especially for food products, also supports the growth of local and regional brands. However, securing retail space remains a pressing challenge.

In cities like Delhi, with approximately **25,000 medium-sized grocery stores contributing 60-70%** of the market, the role of Kiranas as connectors between brands and consumers becomes clear. Personal interviews with over **1,000 Kirana retailers highlight their dedication in managing operations**, dealing with distributors, and maintaining customer relationships, despite the limitations of their modest shop spaces.

The challenges faced by Kirana owners, such as space constraints, competition, and adapting to modern retail trends, are evident. Engaging with these retailers to understand their pain points is crucial for entrepreneurs aiming to develop innovative solutions to protect and enhance their businesses.

By focusing on medium-sized stores, generating monthly revenues of **INR 5–10 lakhs**, this study sheds light on the intricate dynamics of the Kirana ecosystem, offering insights into the perseverance and resourcefulness of these essential contributors to the Indian economy.

Challenges Faced by Kirana Store Owners

1. **Space Constraint:**Most Kirana stores are small, often less than 150 square feet. This limits their ability to stock and display a variety of products effectively.

2. **Improper Product Assortment:**Due to lack of space and market research, they often fail to offer the right mix of products. This impacts their ability to meet customer preferences.

3. **Hygiene Issues:** Maintaining cleanliness is difficult for small stores. Poor hygiene may drive customers away.

4. **Poor Time Management:** Store owners struggle to manage their time while buying or sourcing products. This can lead to shortages or overstocking.

5. **Decreasing Footfall:** With modern retail and online shopping options growing, fewer customers visit Kirana stores, reducing their income.

6. **Mishandling of Product Expiry:** Many store owners cannot properly track expiry dates, leading to losses from expired goods.

7. **Communication Gap:** A lack of communication between companies and retailers often results in missed opportunities for promotions or new products.

8. **Competition from Big Stores:** Large retail chains and walk-through stores offer a better shopping experience and wider variety, posing stiff competition.

9. **Changes in Consumer Behaviour:** Customers now prefer convenience, modern retail stores, and online platforms, impacting Kirana stores.

10. **Manpower Issues:** Most Kirana stores are run by families. Finding and managing additional staff is a major challenge.

11. **Limited Promotions and Offers:** Many manufacturers do not provide adequate promotional materials or discounts, making it harder for Kirana stores to attract customers.

12. **High Density of Kirana Stores:** Too many stores in one area create intense competition and reduce profits for

individual stores.

13. **Younger Generations Moving Away**: Many young family members are not interested in continuing the Kirana business, threatening its future.

14. **Lack of IT Adoption**: Most stores do not use modern tools like POS systems or computerised billing. This affects efficiency and inventory management.

15. **Limited Working Capital**: With restricted funds, store owners find it hard to expand or improve their business.

16. **Compliance with Food Safety Regulations**: Adhering to food safety laws is challenging, especially for perishable goods.

17. **Resistance to Bookkeeping**: Many store owners avoid maintaining proper financial records, leading to inefficiencies and difficulty in managing their business.

18. **Lack of Market Knowledge**: Limited access to market trends and consumer insights makes it harder for Kirana stores to adapt to changes.

19. **No Centralised Body**: Kirana retailers lack a collective organisation to protect their interests and represent them.

20. **Difficulty in Accessing Banking Facilities**: Without proper records, store owners cannot access loans or credit facilities, which limits growth.

Negative Views from Professionals

Some professionals have expressed critical opinions about Kirana stores:

- Kirana stores are seen as outdated and unable to compete with modern retail formats.
- They are criticised for poor hygiene and limited adoption of technology.

- High store density is viewed as unsustainable for long-term growth.
- Professionals feel that the younger generation abandoning the business adds to the uncertainty.

Unfortunately, some professionals have used such negative and demeaning language to describe kirana retailers. These small, family-run businesses are the backbone of the Indian retail industry, providing essential goods and services to millions of people across the country. They play a vital role in supporting local economies and ensuring that everyone has access to essential items.

The comments made by these professionals are not only insensitive but also inaccurate. Kirana retailers are not dinosaurs or relics of the past. They are adapting and evolving to meet the changing needs of consumers. They are embracing technology, offering a wider range of products, and providing better customer service.

We should be celebrating the contributions of Kirana retailers, not denigrating them. They are an important part of India's economy and society, and they deserve our respect and support

Two years back , I had a conversation with a senior executive at Walmart, who mentioned their plans to develop a retail-oriented model where they would provide various products from centralized centres and create credit lines with banks or financial institutions. They are already offering volume purchase discounts, QPS, and other incentives to retailers, with their sales teams actively taking orders from retailers. However, a major challenge remains the credit facility that retailers currently receive from traditional distributors.

After extensive analysis and working on this project since 2009, I have not found a comprehensive solution to protect their businesses. In a market where big retail players are opening stores in nearly every corner, most retailers with resources and vision are transforming their stores into modern outlets.

I have a plan for how they can be saved from such intense competition and what kind of solutions will work for them. During 2012, my concept, 'Pragati,' was at the business model stage and I was looking for investors who could spare 15 minutes to review my business plan. This model is particularly suitable for companies like Flipkart, Amazon, Reliance etc. or those looking to transition from offline to online retail. The franchise model will provide a uniform name for unorganized retailers, granting them access to the market. They will have the capability to attract consumers to their stores, and brands will eagerly showcase their products or secure dynamic shelf space. More consumers will be able to place orders at their nearby stores, with deliveries within 15 minutes, offering speed and convenience. There are numerous revenue streams to explore in this model.

While external concerns are evident, there are inner flaws that remain hidden

In India's retail sector, the story of Kirana stores is both inspiring and challenging. These small, family-run shops face tough competition from large retail chains and e-commerce platforms. They also need to modernise to keep up with changing times. Despite these difficulties, Kirana stores show great resilience and creativity as they adapt to new ways of doing business.

This chapter highlights the opportunities Kirana retailers have to expand their product range, offer new services, and use technology to improve operations and customer experience. It also discusses the role of government policies and regulations in shaping the future of these stores. These rules can significantly affect how these small businesses operate and grow.

India's retail sector is still largely unorganised compared to Western countries. Running a Kirana store in today's semi-modern India is not easy. Changing consumer habits and economic shifts have led to the rise of modern retail formats. However, traditional Kirana stores remain strong despite these changes.

Even though large retail chains and e-commerce companies have grown, Kirana stores continue to play a crucial role. They are important for brands as they connect with customers in both urban and rural areas.

Kirana retailers face many challenges. These include limited space, lack of variety in products, hygiene issues, and competition from larger stores. They also struggle with changing consumer preferences and limited adoption of technology. Additionally, many young people from these families are not interested in continuing the business.

Other problems include compliance with food safety laws, lack of proper bookkeeping, limited market knowledge, and absence of a central organisation to support them. Access to credit and banking facilities is also difficult for many due to poor record-keeping.

Despite these challenges, the future of Kirana stores is filled with opportunities. If these problems are addressed, Kirana stores can continue to thrive and remain a key part of India's retail landscape. New solutions, better policies, and increased collaboration can ensure their relevance in the fast-changing Indian market.

Opportunities for Kirana Retailers with Examples

1. **Personalised Customer Service:** Kirana stores know their customers personally, which allows them to offer tailored services. For example, a Kirana owner might remember a customer's usual shopping list and ensure those items are always stocked. If a customer regularly buys a specific brand of tea, the store can prioritise keeping it in stock, building customer loyalty.

2. **Local Sourcing and Fresh Products:** By sourcing vegetables and fruits from nearby farms, Kirana stores can offer fresher items than big chains. For instance, a Kirana store in a rural area can sell locally grown organic produce, attracting health-conscious buyers who prefer fresh and natural food.

3. **Speciality Products:** Kirana stores can focus on stocking region-specific or cultural products that larger chains often overlook. For instance, during festive seasons like Diwali, stocking items like homemade sweets, diyas, or traditional ingredients can draw in customers looking for authentic products.

4. **Quick Adaptation to Trends :** Kirana stores can easily introduce trending items like millet-based snacks, plant-based milk, or health drinks that customers are beginning to demand. For example, if a health trend emerges in the area, the Kirana store can stock such items quickly compared to a supermarket chain.

5. **Using Technology:** Adopting POS (Point of Sale) systems allows Kirana stores to track sales and inventory more efficiently. For example, stores can use mobile payment apps like Paytm or UPI for seamless transactions, making shopping convenient for tech-savvy customers.

6. **Partnerships with Local Suppliers:** By collaborating with local dairies or bakeries, Kirana stores can offer fresh milk, curd, and bread. For instance, a Kirana store

partnering with a local bakery can provide freshly baked goods every morning, differentiating itself from larger retailers.

7. **Offering More Services:** Kirana stores can introduce home delivery services using WhatsApp orders. For example, a working professional can text their grocery list to the Kirana store and have it delivered at their convenience, saving time and effort.

8. **Connecting with the Community:** Participating in local events, such as sponsoring a school sports day or setting up stalls during a festival, helps Kirana stores strengthen community bonds. For instance, offering discounts during local temple celebrations can attract more customers.

9. **Private Labels:** Launching store-brand items like spices, pickles, or pulses under their label can increase profits. For example, a Kirana store can package its brand of turmeric powder, highlighting its freshness and quality.

10. **Better Supply Chain Management:** Kirana stores can work with distributors to ensure timely deliveries and reduce stock wastage. For instance, an efficient supply chain can help the store avoid overstocking perishables like milk, which can otherwise lead to losses.

11. **Digital Marketing** : By creating a social media page, Kirana stores can promote offers and discounts. For example, a post about "Buy 1 Get 1 Free" on popular snack brands during the IPL season can drive footfall.

12. **Loyalty Programs** : Offering loyalty cards or points systems encourages repeat visits. For example, a Kirana store can provide a free product or discount after a customer completes a certain number of purchases.

13. **Understanding Customers Through Data** : Analysing data from sales can help Kirana stores stock the right

products. For instance, if the data shows high demand for instant noodles and soft drinks during exams, the store can stockpile these items in advance.

14. **Group Purchasing** : Kirana stores in the same locality can form a group to buy goods in bulk at lower prices. For example, if five stores collectively purchase rice sacks, they can negotiate discounts with the supplier, reducing costs.

15. **Eco-Friendly Practices** : Kirana stores can use cloth bags or biodegradable packaging instead of plastic. For example, a store offering free cloth bags with purchases above ₹500 can attract eco-conscious customers.

16. **Quality and Certification** : Displaying food safety certifications can build trust. For example, a Kirana store selling packaged pulses with an FSSAI-certified label can assure customers about the product's quality.

17. **Staff Training** : Training employees to greet customers warmly and handle queries efficiently can improve customer satisfaction. For example, teaching staff to assist elderly customers with their shopping bags can create goodwill.

18. **Improving the Store Layout** : Organising shelves neatly and ensuring clear signage can enhance the shopping experience. For example, having separate sections for daily essentials, snacks, and personal care items makes it easier for customers to locate products.

19. **Listening to Customer Feedback** : Kirana stores can place a suggestion box or ask for feedback directly. For example, if customers request sugar-free biscuits, the store can start stocking them to meet demand.

20. **Strong Branding** : A consistent logo, colour theme, and tagline can make a Kirana store memorable. For

instance, branding a store as "Fresh Mart – Your Neighbourhood Grocer" creates a sense of reliability and connection with the local community.

By tapping into these opportunities, Kirana stores can compete effectively with modern retail formats. Examples like personalised services, quick adaptation, and local sourcing demonstrate their potential. With proper planning and execution, they can carve a significant niche in the retail market.

--==--

SIX

SUPPLY CHAIN AND SOURCING

The procurement and sourcing strategies, inventory management systems, and supplier relationships of Kirana retailers in India form a dynamic subject that underpins their operational success. Kirana retailers employ a multifaceted approach to procure products, ranging from local and regional suppliers to wholesale markets and eB2B startups. Effective inventory management is crucial, involving strategies like just-in-time inventory, stock rotation, categorization, and the use of technology.

These retailers nurture essential relationships with mandi traders, eB2B startups, and traditional wholesalers, ensuring a continuous supply chain. This subject reflects the adaptability of Kirana stores in embracing technology, local sourcing, and efficient inventory practices while maintaining strong ties with their supplier network. It showcases the critical role of Kirana stores in the Indian retail landscape and their ability to cater to the diverse needs of customers in a rapidly changing market.

Kirana retailers manage their procurement and sourcing strategies, inventory management, and relationships with various suppliers

The grocery supply chain channel encompasses a journey from the brand to C&F agents, super stockists, distributors, mandi traders, and wholesalers, with the addition of eB2B platforms connecting businesses. Products flow from manufacturers through intermediaries to retailers, including supermarkets and online platforms. Efficient logistics, strong relationships, and optimal operations at each step are crucial for success in India's dynamic grocery retail market, requiring a strategic approach from your startup.

Procurement and Sourcing Strategies:

1. **Local and Regional Suppliers**: Many Kirana stores rely on local and regional suppliers for sourcing products. These suppliers provide a range of items, from fresh produce to packaged goods. By sourcing locally, Kirana retailers can often negotiate favorable terms and maintain a consistent supply.

2. **Wholesale Markets (Mandi)**: Kirana stores may also procure products from wholesale markets or "mandis." These markets serve as hubs for the trade of agricultural and other commodities. Kirana retailers visit mandis to purchase bulk quantities of items, particularly fresh produce and staples.

3. **eB2B Startups**: The digital era has ushered in eB2B (e-commerce for business) startups that cater specifically to Kirana stores. These platforms connect Kirana retailers with suppliers and wholesalers, providing an online marketplace for sourcing a wide range of products.

Reference: <u>Financial Express - "The rise of eB2B startups"</u>

1. **Traditional Distributors**: Many Kirana retailers have established relationships with traditional distributors who supply products on a regular basis. These distributors serve as intermediaries between manufacturers and retailers, ensuring a smooth flow of goods.

5. **Price Cutters and Opportunist Suppliers:** Some Kirana retailers engage with suppliers who offer discounted rates or special deals. These suppliers may include manufacturers with excess inventory or traders looking to clear stock. While these opportunities can lead to cost savings, they require careful negotiation and judgment to ensure the quality and authenticity of products. Many traders and retail chains take advantage of modern trade arrangements offered by brands. They engage in price-cutting within the general trade sector due to the competitive pricing offered to them by these brands. Products from companies like HUL, P&G, Bikaji, Indiagate, Aashirvad Atta, Godrej No 1 Soap, Tata Tea, Tata Salt, and other demand-driven brands have a strong presence in the market, primarily fueled by opportunistic suppliers.

Inventory Management System: Effective inventory management is crucial for Kirana stores to maintain product availability while minimizing carrying costs.

1. **Just-In-Time Inventory**: Some Kirana stores employ a just-in-time (JIT) inventory system. This system involves ordering and receiving products only as they are needed,

reducing excess stock and storage costs.

2. **Stock Rotation**: Kirana retailers practice stock rotation to ensure older products are sold before newer ones. This minimizes waste and preserves product freshness.

3. **Categorization and Shelving**: Products are categorized and shelved strategically to optimize space and make it easier for customers to find what they need.

4. **Use of Technology**: Many Kirana stores now use inventory management software and point-of-sale (POS) systems to track sales, manage inventory levels, and automate reordering when stock is low.

Reference: The Times of India - "Small shops reinvent to stay relevant"

Relationships with Suppliers: Kirana retailers nurture relationships with various suppliers to ensure a smooth supply chain.

1. **Mandi Traders**: Kirana stores often have close ties with traders from local mandis. These relationships are vital for sourcing fresh produce and staple goods.

2. **eB2B Startups**: Kirana retailers who use eB2B platforms build relationships with these startups. These platforms provide a streamlined way to source a wide range of products and offer credit facilities. Examples are Udaan, Jumbotail, Shopkirana, Kiranaking, Apnaclub, Elasticrun etc.

3. **Wholesalers**: Traditional wholesalers play a significant role in the Kirana retail ecosystem. Kirana stores build enduring relationships with wholesalers to access a diverse range of goods.

Reference: YourStory - "How Kirana stores are using tech to go hyperlocal"

In conclusion, Kirana retailers in India manage their procurement and sourcing through a combination of local suppliers, wholesale markets, eB2B startups, and traditional distributors. Effective inventory management, technology adoption, and careful product shelving contribute to efficient operations. Strong relationships with mandi traders, eB2B startups, and wholesalers are essential to ensure a steady supply of goods, making Kirana stores a vital and adaptable part of the Indian retail sector.

--==--

SEVEN

Technology Adoption and Transforming Programs

We take a closer look at the profound impact of technology on India's Kirana retail ecosystem. The adoption of technology has ushered in a new era, improving efficiency, enhancing customer satisfaction, and enabling Kirana retailers to stay competitive in a rapidly changing market. This transformation is driven by the use of mobile apps, Point of Sale (POS) systems, and inventory management tools. Additionally, the integration of Kirana stores into the e-commerce landscape has reshaped the retail industry.

Innovative startups have been instrumental in equipping Kirana retailers with the resources and expertise needed to harness the power of technology for business growth. Technology has fundamentally altered how these neighborhood stores operate. Mobile apps now play a critical role, helping Kirana retailers manage stock, interact with customers, and streamline daily operations.

In the eB2B (business-to-business) sector, supply chain and distribution aggregators such as Udaan, ElasticRun, ApnaClub, ShopKirana, KiranaKing, and Jumbotail have been trailblazers. These platforms connect Kirana retailers with suppliers digitally, offering access to a wide range of products, better price negotiations, and simplified ordering processes. By leveraging these tools, small retailers can run their businesses more efficiently and remain relevant in today's competitive market.

The Role of Technology in Kirana Retail: Technology has evolved from being a luxury to a necessity for Kirana retailers. It plays a multifaceted role, from simplifying daily operations to enhancing the overall shopping experience. With the aid of mobile apps, Kirana retailers can digitize their businesses, track inventory, monitor sales, and even offer personalized deals to customers. This transformation has made Kirana stores more competitive and adaptable, ensuring their survival in a rapidly changing market.

Use of Mobile Apps, POS Systems, and Inventory Tools: Mobile apps designed for Kirana retailers have become vital assets. These apps facilitate inventory management, order placement, and customer engagement. Prominent names like Dukaan, Vyapar, and OkCredit & Snabizz offer features tailored to the specific needs of Kirana retailers. In addition to mobile apps, Point of Sale (POS) systems have streamlined the billing process and simplified financial management. These tools help Kirana retailers maintain accurate records and manage cash flow efficiently. Inventory management tools have further improved stock control, reducing waste and ensuring products are always in stock when needed.

Online Presence and E-Commerce Integration: The rise of e-commerce has not left Kirana retailers untouched. Many Kirana stores now have an online presence, either through their websites or via e-commerce platforms like Amazon and Flipkart. These digital storefronts allow them to tap into a broader customer base and cater to the growing demand for online shopping. Moreover, e-commerce integration has enabled Kirana stores to access a wider range of products and compete with larger retailers effectively.

Initiatives by Pioneering Startups: In the last decade, several startups have taken the initiative to empower Kirana retailers with technology. Companies like Udaan and Jumbotail have been instrumental in bridging the gap between Kirana retailers and suppliers through their eB2B platforms. These startups have not only provided access to a vast array of products but have also educated Kirana retailers on how to use technology effectively. By offering user-friendly apps and technical support, they have revolutionized the way Kirana stores do business.

In conclusion, technology adoption has ushered in a new era for Kirana retail, redefining the way these stores operate, engage with customers, and manage their sourcing. The integration of mobile apps, POS systems, and e-commerce has empowered Kirana retailers to compete in an evolving market. Pioneering startups have played a crucial role in equipping Kirana retailers with the tools and knowledge required to thrive in this tech-driven retail landscape. The journey of Kirana retail is marked by innovation, adaptability, and resilience, making it an integral part of India's retail future.

Transformation program initiatives by the Startups

1. Kirana King:

- **Founders**: Anup K. Kumar, Deepak Dusad, Madan K Gandam & Balwant Singh Rana (myself)
- **Model**: Kirana King operates through the RAAS (Retail As A Service) model, centralizing supply and marketing for Kirana stores.
- **Impact**: Kirana King has successfully transformed 250 stores in Jaipur, unifying them under a single brand, providing operational support, and enhancing the customer shopping experience.
- **One Umbrella solution of Private Label** : Kirana King provides consumer pack and bulk pack in main Staple segment. It means quality products in main staples from one umbrella. This increase margin and quality consumers reach to the stores.

2. Gully Network:

- **Co-Founder**: Ajay Nain
- **Initiative**: Gully Network focuses on digitizing and modernizing mid-sized Kirana stores, aiming to tap into a $25 billion untapped market segment.

3. Express Store:

- **Founder**: Apoorv Jain
- **Model**: Express Store offers a 360-degree solution for Kirana stores, helping them modernize and provide a better shopping experience while ensuring profitable operations.

4. Smart Kirana by METRO Wholesale:

- **Initiative:** METRO Wholesale's Smart Kirana aims to transform old and closed-format shops into modern supermarkets, providing a wide range of products and enhancing the retail experience for customers.

5. 1K Kirana:

- **Founders:** Sangeetesh Sharma, Sachin Sharma
- **Business Model:** 1K Kirana partners with offline Kirana shops to organize and modernize them, offering a broader range of products and services to customers.

6. Walmart's Mera Kirana:

- Walmart's initiative focuses on empowering Kirana retailers with technology and supply chain support to enhance their operations.

7. Jio's Smart Kirana:

- **Initiative:** Jio, a subsidiary of Reliance Industries, aims to transform traditional Kirana stores into "Smart Kiranas" by providing digital solutions and supply chain support.

8. Amazon:

- Amazon has launched various programs and initiatives to partner with Kirana stores and empower them with technology for a more streamlined and efficient business.

9. DealShare:

- **Initiative:** DealShare operates in the online grocery retail space, partnering with local Kirana stores and organizing them to provide discounted products to consumers.

The efforts of startups and corporate initiatives to transform and empower Kirana retailers have faced several challenges that have, in some cases, limited their success. Here are some reasons why these endeavors may have encountered resistance or limitations from Kirana retailers:

1. Resistance to Change:

- Kirana retailers often have well-established, traditional business practices. They may resist changes that disrupt their existing routines or require them to adopt new technologies and processes. Many Kirana retailers are hesitant to embrace digital solutions, as these may seem complex or unfamiliar.

2. Lack of Trust:

- Building trust is crucial in any partnership. Kirana retailers may have reservations about the intentions and reliability of startups or corporate initiatives. Concerns about data privacy, control over their business, and long-term commitments can lead to a lack of trust.

3. Financial Constraints:

- Many Kirana retailers operate on thin profit margins and limited resources. The cost of adopting new technology or changing business processes can be a barrier, especially if they don't see immediate benefits or a clear return on investment.

4. Training and Education:

- Kirana retailers may lack the necessary training and education to effectively use new technology or adapt to modern business practices. The absence of adequate training programs can hinder their ability to embrace change.

5. Fear of Losing Autonomy:

- Kirana retailers value their independence and autonomy in decision-making. Some may be concerned that partnering with startups or corporate initiatives could lead to a loss of control over their business, impacting their decision-making freedom.

6. Localization and Personalization:

- Kirana retailers often have a deep understanding of the local community and customer preferences. They may feel that centralized solutions offered by startups do not adequately cater to the unique needs of their local customer base.

7. Competition:

- In some cases, Kirana retailers may perceive startups or corporate initiatives as potential competitors. This perception can create resistance to collaboration, as retailers may believe that these entities are trying to replace them rather than support them.

8. Inadequate Communication and Support:

- Startups and corporate initiatives may not effectively communicate the benefits of their solutions or provide adequate support to Kirana retailers during the adoption process. This can leave retailers feeling unsupported and frustrated.

9. Cultural and Language Barriers:

- Kirana retailers, especially in smaller towns and rural areas, may face challenges related to language and cultural differences when dealing with startups that have a more urban or tech-savvy focus.

10. External Market Forces:

- The presence of large retail chains and e-commerce giants in the market can create intense competition for Kirana retailers. While startups aim to empower them, the dominance of these external market forces can limit their impact.

In conclusion, the transformation of Kirana retailers by startups and corporate initiatives is a complex process that requires addressing the unique challenges and concerns of these small businesses. Successful initiatives must focus on building trust, offering relevant and localized solutions, and providing comprehensive support and education to Kirana retailers. The resistance or limitations faced by these initiatives should be viewed as opportunities to better understand the needs and aspirations of Kirana retailers and tailor solutions accordingly.

These startup initiatives and corporate programs aim to empower Kirana retailers, transform their traditional business models, and enhance the customer shopping experience. They focus on digitization, centralization of supply chains, modernization, and offering a wider range of products. These efforts are essential in bridging the gap between traditional Kirana stores and the modern retail landscape, ensuring the continued relevance and growth of Kirana retail in India.

--==--

EIGHT

CUSTOMER ENGAGEMENT AND SERVICE

In this chapter, we explore the essence of customer engagement and service within the vibrant world of Kirana retail. The remarkable success of these neighbourhood stores lies in their unique ability to nurture and maintain a loyal customer base. The personal touch provided by Kirana stores fosters strong relationships, making them stand out in a competitive landscape dominated by large retail chains. At the core of this relationship-driven model is an unwavering foundation of trust. Moreover, a growing number of companies are now dedicated to helping Kirana retailers elevate their customer engagement and service strategies, ensuring their cherished place in the hearts of consumers.

Kirana retailers particularly excel in customer engagement and service for several compelling reasons:

1. **Local Presence and Community Integration**: Kirana retailers are deeply ingrained in their local communities. They often serve the same customers over extended periods, even generations. This longstanding local presence allows them to develop personal relationships and understand the specific needs and preferences of their customers.
2. **Personalized Service**: Kirana retailers are known for their personalized service. Shopkeepers often know their customers by name and are familiar with their shopping habits. This level of intimacy allows them to provide tailored recommendations and a sense of belonging, making customers feel valued.
3. **Flexibility and Adaptability**: Kirana retailers are agile and can swiftly adapt to changing customer demands. They can adjust their product offerings, pricing, and promotions to align with local preferences. This adaptability ensures that they can consistently meet customer expectations.
4. **Credit Facilities**: Many Kirana retailers extend credit to regular customers, allowing them to make purchases even when they are short on cash. This flexibility is particularly crucial for lower-income households, fostering a sense of trust and reliability.
5. **Cultural and Social Significance**: Kirana stores often serve as community hubs, where people not only shop but also engage in social interactions and exchange information. This social dimension reinforces the relationship between Kirana retailers and their customers.
6. **Proximity and Convenience**: Kirana retailers are typically located within or near residential areas, ensuring easy access for consumers. The convenience

of shopping at a nearby store is a significant driver of customer loyalty.

7. **Competitive Pricing:** Kirana retailers often offer competitive pricing, leveraging their local sourcing and supply chain connections. This attracts price-conscious customers and helps build trust.

8. **Long-Term Commitment:** Kirana retailers are often family-owned businesses passed down through generations. This long-term commitment to the neighbourhood fosters a strong sense of trust and stability.

9. **Community Engagement:** Kirana retailers actively engage with their local communities through sponsorships, events, and other initiatives. This engagement reinforces their position as community pillars and enhances customer loyalty.

Kirana retailers' strength in customer engagement and service is rooted in their local presence, personalized approach, flexibility, and deep community connections. These factors create a unique and compelling value proposition that fosters enduring relationships with customers.

Building and Retaining a Loyal Customer Base: Central to Kirana Retail's success is the art of building and retaining a loyal customer base. It goes beyond mere transactions; it's about forging genuine connections with the community. Companies such as Capillary Technologies and Loyalty Solutions have provided innovative solutions that empower Kirana retailers to launch loyalty programs, reward their customers, and gain insights into purchasing behaviours. These programs foster a sense of belonging, enticing customers to return, knowing they are valued. Loyalty in

Kirana retail transcends mere discounts; it's a commitment to the neighborhood, and Kirana stores have mastered this art. Various Startups like Okcredit, Vyapar, Khatabook build some interaction tools where retailers can publish their inventories to their end consumers or can send offers on WhatsApp or SMS.

Personalized Customer Service: One of the significant distinctions between Kirana stores and larger retailers is the level of personalized customer service they offer. Companies like Zoho CRM and Freshdesk provide Kirana retailers with customer relationship management tools that enable them to understand their patrons better. By capturing preferences and purchase history, Kirana retailers can offer tailored recommendations and experiences. This personal touch transcends mere transactions and builds lasting relationships.

The Role of Trust and Relationships: Trust is the lifeblood of Kirana Retail. Unlike impersonal big-box retailers, customers know their Kirana shopkeeper by name, and vice versa. This trust is rooted in the local community and is the driving force behind the enduring success of Kirana Retail. Companies like Trade Promoters and V-Share play a vital role in helping Kirana retailers manage their relationships with suppliers, ensuring timely and reliable inventory replenishment. Trust extends not only to customers but also to the network of wholesalers and distributors that Kirana retailers rely on.

Initiatives by Pioneering Companies:Several companies have recognized the unique needs of Kirana retailers and offered solutions to enhance customer engagement and service. Capillary Technologies, a pioneer in this field, provides a range of customer engagement and loyalty solutions, empowering Kirana retailers to create personalized rewards programs that resonate with their local customer base. Zoho CRM equips Kirana retailers with robust customer relationship management tools, while Freshdesk enhances customer support capabilities, enabling them to provide top-notch service. Trade Promoters and V-Share assist Kirana retailers in managing supplier relationships, ensuring a seamless inventory chain.

In conclusion, the essence of Kirana retail lies in the deep-rooted relationships, trust, and loyalty that these neighbourhood stores cultivate. They are not just places to shop; they are pillars of the community. Innovative solutions from companies specializing in customer engagement, loyalty programs, and supplier management empower Kirana retailers to further strengthen their bond with customers and suppliers alike. In the age of digitization, Kirana Retail thrives on the age-old values of trust and personalization, making it a cherished institution in the retail landscape.

References: Capillary Technologies, Loyalty Solutions, Zoho CRM, Freshdesk, Trade Promoters, V-Share

--=--

NINE

FINANCIAL MANAGEMENT & SHIELD

Financial management is the cornerstone of success and long-term sustainability for Kirana retailers. In an ever-evolving retail environment, managing finances wisely is essential for these small neighborhood stores to thrive. Here we will learn about the key aspects of financial management specifically designed to meet the unique needs of Kirana retailers. We will cover budgeting and financial planning, setting the right pricing strategies and profit margins, and the critical task of managing cash flow effectively.

For Kirana retailers, financial management is often a balancing act, as many operate on tight margins with limited resources. They must ensure that every rupee spent adds value to their business while keeping costs in check. Effective budgeting helps them allocate resources efficiently, while solid pricing strategies allow them to remain competitive yet profitable. Furthermore, cash flow management is key to ensuring that they can meet day-to-day expenses, stock up on inventory, and respond to market changes without financial strain. Ultimately, the success of a Kirana store is tied to its ability to navigate these financial challenges with foresight and precision.

Budgeting and Financial Planning: Budgeting and financial planning are the keystones of Kirana retail financial management. They serve as the guiding lights that navigate these businesses through the volatile waters of the market. Budgeting involves the methodical allocation of resources, forecasting income, and controlling expenses over a designated period. It's where Kirana retailers estimate costs, sales, and profits. Financial planning extends beyond budgeting, focusing on strategies and action plans to actualize financial objectives.

To facilitate effective budgeting and financial planning, Kirana retailers increasingly turn to digital tools and software solutions. Companies such as Tally Solutions, Zoho Books, and QuickBooks offer platforms that streamline financial management. These tools simplify the process, making it more accessible to retailers. They offer features like expense tracking, income prediction, and financial statement generation, enabling Kirana retailers to maintain financial discipline.

Pricing Strategies and Profit Margins: Pricing strategies and profit margins are pivotal for Kirana retailers, often competing with larger retail chains. Setting the right prices while safeguarding profitability is both an art and a science. Kirana retailers must navigate the intricacies of market dynamics, consumer preferences, and competitive pricing strategies.

In the digital age, technology-driven solutions play a vital role in setting competitive prices while preserving profit margins. POS systems with price optimization features empower Kirana retailers to dynamically adjust prices in response to market trends. Companies like Shopify, Lightspeed, and MARG ERP provide retail management software equipped with pricing strategies tailored to the unique needs of Kirana retailers.

Managing Cash Flow: Cash flow management, the lifeblood of any business, holds particular importance for Kirana retailers. These neighborhood stores rely on a consistent cash flow to meet daily expenses and keep operations running smoothly. Effective cash flow management involves monitoring income, outflows, and the timing of financial transactions.

Kirana retailers find support in modern financial tools, mobile banking applications, accounting software, and POS systems. Mobile banking apps offered by reputable financial institutions such as HDFC Bank, ICICI Bank, and Axis Bank facilitate digital payments, simplifying financial transactions and tracking. Accounting software solutions, including Zoho Books and QuickBooks, feature functionalities designed to assist Kirana retailers in cash flow management.

Fintech Companies and Startups: Several fintech companies and startups have recognized the unique financial needs of Kirana retailers and are actively providing solutions:

1. **Khatabook**: Khatabook is a startup that offers digital ledger and bookkeeping solutions specifically tailored for small businesses, including Kirana stores. It simplifies tracking credit, managing accounts, and

maintaining financial records.

2. **Vyapar**: Vyapar is another fintech startup that provides accounting and inventory management software for small businesses. Kirana retailers can efficiently handle invoicing, expense tracking, and inventory management through this platform.
3. **OkCredit**: OkCredit is a digital ledger app designed for small businesses. It assists Kirana retailers in recording credit transactions, managing ledgers, and ensuring transparency in financial dealings.

Startups Providing Channel Funding: Channel funding, which involves providing financial support to supply chain partners, is crucial for Kirana retailers. Several startups are active in this domain:

1. **Jai Kisan**: Jai Kisan is a fintech startup that focuses on channel financing for small retailers, including Kirana stores. It offers credit and working capital solutions to enhance their business operations.
2. **Lendingkart**: Lendingkart is a fintech company that provides working capital loans to small businesses. Kirana retailers can leverage Lendingkart's services for channel funding and managing their financial needs.

We are analyzing the crucial aspects that empower Kirana retailers to maintain financial control and ensure the sustainability of their businesses. Budgeting and financial planning are vital, and in this pursuit, several fintech companies and startups, such as Khatabook and OkCredit, offer digital ledger solutions to streamline accounting and bookkeeping. These tools simplify tracking credit, managing accounts, and maintaining financial records, a necessity for small businesses. Additionally, working capital and cash flow management are addressed by the likes of Udaan and Jumbotail, B2B e-commerce platforms offering channel financing to Kirana retailers. These services provide access to much-needed funds and financial support for enhancing business operations. Channel funding is further facilitated by startups like Jai Kisan and Lendingkart, which specialize in offering credit and working capital solutions tailored to the unique needs of small retailers. By embracing these financial tools and collaborations with fintech providers and B2B platforms, Kirana retailers strengthen their financial resilience and navigate the complexities of the retail market with greater ease and confidence.

--==--

TEN

SUSTAINABILITY AND SOCIAL IMPACT

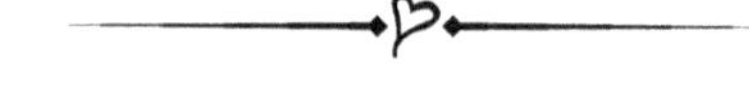

In the fast-paced world of Kirana retail, where daily transactions and customer interactions define the rhythm of life, there is an underlying sense of responsibility that goes beyond simply selling goods. Kirana stores are often small, with unassuming storefronts, but they play a much more important role than just providing products. They are at the heart of their local communities, shaping the way people shop and connect with their neighbourhoods.

The owners of Kirana stores understand the value of building relationships. Over time, they establish trust with their customers, offering a personal touch that larger retail chains cannot match. Customers feel more than just shoppers – they feel like part of a family. This bond is not just about customer service, it's about being a reliable and consistent part of everyday life.

At the same time, many Kirana retailers are making conscious efforts to embrace sustainability. They are increasingly mindful of their environmental impact, whether it's by reducing plastic use, sourcing local products, or adopting eco-friendly practices. These small but significant steps help reduce waste and promote responsible consumption in their communities.

Additionally, Kirana retailers often support local farmers, producers, and small businesses by sourcing products directly from them. This not only ensures fresh and high-quality products for customers but also strengthens the local economy. By supporting local businesses, Kirana retailers contribute to the growth and development of their community.

Thus, while Kirana stores may appear modest on the outside, they hold deep values of sustainability, social responsibility, and community connection. Their impact is far-reaching, making them an essential pillar of both the local economy and society.

Sustainable Practices in Kirana Retail: These unassuming stores have quietly and steadfastly integrated sustainable practices into their daily operations. While this commitment might not always be loudly proclaimed, it is undoubtedly present. Many Kirana retailers have recognized the importance of stocking locally sourced produce. By doing so, they support local farmers and reduce the carbon footprint associated with transportation. Additionally, Kirana store owners are conscious of minimizing plastic usage. Some have taken commendable steps by offering organic and eco-friendly products on their shelves. This not only aligns with the growing awareness of sustainable living among consumers but also reflects the ethical choices made by these retailers.

Kirana Stores as Community Hubs:

But Kirana stores are far more than mere places of trade. They represent the very heartbeats of communities. In these modest establishments, relationships are not just transactions; they are bonds that are forged over time. It's where neighbors meet and greet, where news is exchanged, and where personal connections are nurtured. In a world increasingly characterized by isolation and digital interactions, Kirana stores remain steadfast as physical community hubs. They provide a refuge, a place where the essence of human connection is preserved, where faces are recognized, and names remembered. Amidst the cacophony of modern life, these Kirana stores stand as quiet oases of human interaction and social cohesion.

Social Responsibility and Community Engagement:

The Kirana store owner is not merely a vendor; they are an integral part of the communities they serve. This role goes beyond the act of commerce. It extends into social responsibility and community engagement. Kirana store owners often take on the responsibility of sponsoring local events, contributing to religious festivals, or supporting charitable causes within their communities. Their sense of social responsibility is palpable. They are not detached entities but deeply intertwined with the social fabric of their neighborhoods. In times of need, Kirana retailers are often among the first to extend a helping hand, exemplifying the ethos of "neighbor helping neighbor."

In this chapter, we embark on a journey to explore these often-unseen facets of Kirana retail. Here, we delve into the realm of sustainability, community, and social responsibility. Kirana stores, small and unassuming as they may be, stand not just as pillars of the retail industry but as guardians of tradition and sustainability. Their values are intricately woven into the rich tapestry of Indian society, and their impact extends far beyond their modest storefronts. They are the unsung heroes of sustainability, community, and social cohesion, demonstrating the profound influence of small businesses on the fabric of our society.

While there might not be specific companies that are widely recognized for providing sustainability and social impact services to Kirana stores, there are organizations and initiatives that promote sustainable practices and social responsibility in the retail sector, including Kirana stores. Some of these organizations and initiatives in India include:

1. Confederation of All India Traders (CAIT): CAIT is a prominent trade organization in India that works to promote ethical and sustainable business practices among small retailers, including Kirana stores.
2. Local NGOs and Community Initiatives: Many local non-governmental organizations (NGOs) and community initiatives work with Kirana stores to implement sustainable practices and community engagement. These organizations often collaborate with retailers to reduce plastic usage, promote eco-friendly products, and engage in community-building activities.
3. State and Local Government Initiatives: State and local governments in India often run programs to encourage sustainable practices and social responsibility in the retail sector. These initiatives may include incentives for eco-friendly practices and support for community engagement.
4. FMCG Companies and Brands: Fast-moving consumer goods (FMCG) companies often collaborate with Kirana

stores to promote sustainable products and practices. Brands like HUL, P&G, and others have initiatives related to sustainability and community engagement that may involve Kirana retailers.

5. Digital Platforms and Apps: Digital platforms and apps, such as Khatabook and OkCredit, which you mentioned earlier, may also offer features or guidance related to sustainability and community engagement for Kirana retailers.

While these organizations and initiatives don't directly provide services to Kirana stores in the same way that technology platforms or financial solutions do, they play a role in promoting sustainable practices and social impact in the retail ecosystem, which includes Kirana stores. Retailers may engage with them for guidance, support, and collaboration on these matters.

--==--

ELEVEN
FUTURE TRENDS

As we peer into the crystal ball to anticipate the future of Kirana retail in India, several predictions and emerging trends come into focus. The resilience and adaptability of Kirana stores, combined with the ongoing evolution of the retail landscape, offer promising insights into what lies ahead.

Predictions for the Future of Kirana Retail in India:

1. **Tech Integration:** The integration of technology into Kirana operations will continue to accelerate. Mobile apps, point-of-sale (POS) systems, and digital ledger solutions will become the norm, enabling Kirana store owners to streamline their processes and serve tech-savvy customers efficiently.

2. **Online Presence:** Kirana stores will strengthen their online presence. More of them will adopt e-commerce platforms and engage with customers through digital channels, offering home deliveries and click-and-collect services. This shift towards omnichannel retail will help Kirana stores remain competitive in the digital age.

3. **Sustainability:** The emphasis on sustainability will grow. Kirana stores will increasingly stock organic and eco-friendly products, reducing plastic usage and promoting environmentally responsible choices. This aligns with the rising demand for sustainable and healthy living.

4. **Collaborations:** Kirana retailers will form strategic collaborations with eB2B startups and tech companies to enhance their sourcing, inventory management, and customer engagement. Companies like Udaan, Jumbotail, Khatabook, and OkCredit will play a pivotal role in supporting Kirana store owners in this journey.

5. **Diversification:** Kirana stores will diversify their product offerings. The trend of offering specialty and niche products will expand, catering to specific customer preferences and regional demands.

Emerging Trends and Opportunities:

1. **Channel Financing:** The role of channel financing offered by platforms like Udaan and Jumbotail will become increasingly vital. These services provide Kirana retailers with much-needed working capital, ensuring the smooth operation of their businesses.

2. **Fintech Solutions:** Fintech companies like Khatabook and OkCredit will further revolutionize Kirana store financial management. Digital ledger solutions will simplify accounting, credit tracking, and financial planning, ensuring the financial stability of Kirana businesses.

3. **Community-Centric Approach:** The trend of Kirana stores being community hubs will persist. Owners will engage actively in social responsibility and community

activities, creating a sense of belonging and trust among their customers.

4. **Innovation:** Kirana store owners will continue to innovate. Partnerships with local producers, integration of new technologies, and a focus on customer service will drive their success.

5. **Local Sourcing:** There will be a renewed focus on local sourcing. Kirana stores will forge closer ties with local suppliers and farmers, promoting the 'vocal for local' movement.

The future of Kirana retail in India is poised for transformation, characterized by technology integration, sustainability, and community-centric approaches. As Kirana stores embrace emerging trends and opportunities, they will remain vital pillars of India's retail landscape, continuing to serve diverse customer needs while adapting to changing times.

In the future of Kirana retail in India, the role of traditional distributors, wholesalers, and Mandi traders will undergo significant changes while remaining vital to the ecosystem. Here's a glimpse of their potential roles:

1. Digital Transformation: Traditional distributors and wholesalers will increasingly adopt digital tools and platforms to streamline their operations. They will likely partner with eB2B startups, such as Udaan and Jumbotail, to expand their reach and offer a broader range of products to Kirana retailers. The integration of technology will enhance efficiency in procurement, inventory management, and order processing.

2. Aggregator and Facilitator: Mandi traders will continue to serve as aggregators for fresh produce, connecting farmers with Kirana retailers. However, they may adopt technology-driven solutions to improve supply chain visibility, reduce wastage, and ensure the quality and safety of agricultural products. They could act as facilitators between farmers and retailers, ensuring a more seamless and efficient flow of goods.

3. Local Sourcing and Collaboration: Traditional distributors, wholesalers, and Mandi traders will collaborate with Kirana stores to promote local sourcing. As the 'vocal for local' movement gains momentum, they will play a pivotal role in bridging the gap between local producers and retailers. This collaboration will enhance the availability of fresh and region-specific products in Kirana stores.

4. Supply Chain Innovation: To meet the evolving demands of Kirana retailers, distributors and wholesalers will innovate their supply chain models. They may adopt practices such as demand forecasting, efficient inventory management, and flexible delivery options to cater to the needs of Kirana stores in a dynamic retail landscape.

5. Channel Financing: Distributors and wholesalers will offer channel financing solutions to Kirana retailers to enhance their working capital and business sustainability. They may collaborate with fintech companies to provide financial support to Kirana stores, ensuring a smooth flow of goods and payments.

Overall, the future role of traditional distributors, wholesalers, and Mandi traders in Kirana retail will be one of adaptation and innovation. By embracing technology, focusing on local sourcing, and supporting Kirana retailers with financing and supply chain solutions, these key players in the supply chain will remain indispensable in the evolving Kirana ecosystem. Their ability to evolve with the changing retail landscape will be essential to their continued relevance and success.

The Kirana retail landscape in India is a diverse and dynamic ecosystem. It includes various types of Kirana stores, ranging from traditional to specialty, each catering to unique consumer needs. Ownership models vary, from family-owned businesses to franchises and cooperatives, contributing to the richness of the Kirana landscape.

Business models within Kirana stores have evolved to embrace technology, offering online shopping options and hybrid models that combine traditional and digital services. These stores also serve as essential community hubs, fostering social interactions and community bonds.

Fintech companies like Khatabook and Udaan play a crucial role in financial management, providing tools for budgeting, financial planning, and channel financing. Sustainability and social impact are integral to Kirana stores, as they adopt eco-friendly practices and actively engage with their communities.

Technology adoption, personalized customer service, and the role of eB2B startups are shaping the future of Kirana retail. Traditional distributors and wholesalers are adapting to digital transformation and channel financing to remain relevant in the evolving landscape.

Kirana retail is more than just a way of shopping; it embodies community, adaptability, and sustainability, remaining a cornerstone of the Indian retail sector

--==--

TWELVE

REMEDIES FOR BRANDS – KEYNOTES

The Kirana retailer stands as a pivotal stakeholder, wielding substantial influence in brand-building. Amidst the vast array of brands, they contend with a daily influx of 10-15 new brands courting them through distributors or company sales teams. Time management becomes critical as they navigate this sea of offerings. Fifteen years ago, Kirana retailers were the driving force, instilling confidence in consumers for new product purchases. However, the landscape has shifted with FMCG companies introducing new SKUs, the rise of retail chains, eB2B platforms, and e-commerce, coupled with the surge of local and regional brands challenging national counterparts.

This surge has flooded Kirana stores, grappling with limited space to manage inventory efficiently based on their customer base. Presently, the competitive onslaught from offline retail giants like Dmart and quick commerce platforms such as Blinkit, Zepto, Instamart, and Jiomart poses a formidable challenge, denting the zeal and enthusiasm of Kirana retailers. Their patience wears thin, particularly as the impetus to entertain new brands becomes a daunting task.

Compounding the challenge, distributors lack motivation due to the shrinkage of retailers' business, leading to a lack of interest in onboarding new brands. This predicament raises pertinent questions for new brands aspiring to establish themselves in the retail sphere. Convincing distributors, SS, wholesalers, and Mandi traders to onboard and place products in Kirana retailers' shops becomes a formidable task.

The current scenario prompts an exploration into the reasons behind this trend and how new brands can navigate these challenges to win over Kirana retailers. Moreover, the discussion delves into the potential of Direct-to-Consumer (D2C) as an avenue for brands to reach consumers directly. However, the inquiry extends to scrutinize potential limitations, such as scalability issues, and assesses the impact, recognizing that Kirana retailers remain the linchpin. Without their support, achieving mass presence in the market becomes an uphill task, impacting scalability and long-term profitability.

In a projection for the next five years, the prognosis suggests that brands will encounter increased struggles in securing a respectable place within Kirana retail shops. The evolving dynamics underscore the need for innovative strategies, adaptability, and a keen understanding of the unique challenges faced by Kirana retailers in the ever-changing retail landscape.

Embarking on the journey to understand Kirana dynamics, each strategy represents a step toward forging lasting connections. Just as a ship needs every sail to catch the wind, brands must unfurl these tailored approaches to navigate the vast seas of retail. With a data-driven compass, they chart a course through consumer trends, ensuring each product aligns with the unique currents of Kirana preferences. Crafting local strategies becomes the anchor, grounding the brand in trust and community understanding. Together, these strategies form a resilient vessel, weathering disruptions and ensuring the brand sails smoothly into the heart of Kirana retail success.

The ensuing 30 solutions are poised to assist brands in positioning their products effectively within the Kirana retail landscape

1. Understanding Kirana Dynamics

Understanding Kirana Dynamics" refers to the comprehensive grasp and insight into the operational intricacies, challenges, and unique features of Kirana retailers in the context of the retail ecosystem. This involves a deep understanding of how Kirana retailers operate, manage their inventory, interact with customers, and navigate the daily challenges they face in their business. It also encompasses awareness of the evolving consumer preferences within the specific market served by Kirana retailers. This understanding forms the foundation for tailoring products, strategies, and business approaches to align seamlessly with the dynamic and distinctive nature of Kirana retail.

Brands must delve deep into the intricacies of Kirana retailers' operations, comprehending their challenges and evolving consumer preferences. This insight is crucial for tailoring products and strategies to align with the unique dynamics of the Kirana retail ecosystem.

2. Data-Driven Approach

The concept of a "Data-Driven Approach" involves leveraging the power of data analytics and insights to inform and guide decision-making processes within the context of engaging with Kirana retailers. In this context, brands employ data analytics tools and methodologies to gather, analyze, and interpret relevant data related to consumer trends, market dynamics, and the performance of products in Kirana retail settings. By adopting a data-driven approach, brands can extract valuable insights that empower them to make informed decisions. For Kirana retailers, this means utilizing data to understand consumer preferences, optimize product selection and stocking, and enhance overall efficiency in their operations. This approach allows brands to align their strategies closely with the ever-changing landscape of Kirana retail, ensuring that their products meet the demands and expectations of both retailers and consumers.

Implementing a data-driven approach is imperative. Brands should leverage data analytics to extract valuable insights into consumer trends, empowering Kirana retailers to make informed decisions on product selection and stocking. Example is here:

Imagine "RanaHarvest," a consumer goods brand, aiming to launch a new line of organic snacks tailored for health-conscious consumers through Kirana retailers. To ensure a successful introduction, RanaHarvest adopts a data-driven approach.

a. **Consumer Trend Analysis:** RanaHarvest employs data analytics tools to scrutinize consumer trends in the local market served by Kirana retailers. The data reveals a growing inclination towards organic and healthy snack options.

b. ***Product Selection Optimization:*** Informed by the data insights, RanaHarvest refines its product selection, focusing on creating a line of organic snacks with diverse flavor profiles that align with the specific preferences of the local consumer base.

c. **Stocking Strategies:** The data-driven approach also guides RanaHarvest in determining the optimal stocking strategies for Kirana retailers. By analyzing purchasing patterns and demand forecasts, the brand ensures that the right products are stocked in appropriate quantities, mitigating the risk of overstocking or understocking.

d. **Customized Marketing Campaigns:** Leveraging the data, RanaHarvest tailors its marketing campaigns to resonate with local tastes. For example, if the data indicates a preference for spicy snacks, the marketing messages highlight the bold flavors of the new organic snacks.

e. **Feedback Loop Implementation:** RanaHarvest establishes a feedback loop with Kirana retailers, encouraging them to share insights on product performance and customer reactions. This continuous feedback loop, facilitated by data analytics, allows the brand to make real-time adjustments and improvements.

In this example, the data-driven approach enables RanaHarvest to navigate the complexities of the Kirana retail landscape effectively. By aligning its product offerings and strategies with concrete data insights, the brand increases the likelihood of success in introducing its new line of organic snacks through Kirana retailers.

3. Localized Marketing Strategies

Crafting marketing strategies that resonate with local tastes and preferences is key. Demonstrating a commitment to understanding the community builds trust and ensures the brand aligns seamlessly with the Kirana retail landscape. Examples are:

RanaHarvest recognizes the importance of tailoring its marketing strategies to resonate with local tastes and preferences. Here's how the brand implements localized marketing:

1. **Cultural Sensitivity:** Understanding that cultural nuances play a significant role in consumer behavior, RanaHarvest conducts thorough research on the community served by Kirana retailers. For instance, in a region where festivals hold immense cultural significance, the brand aligns promotional activities with these festivities.

2. **Language Customization:** RanaHarvest ensures that all marketing materials, including brochures and promotional signage, are presented in the local language. This linguistic customization fosters better communication and understanding between the brand and Kirana retailers, enhancing the overall brand-retailer relationship.

3. **Seasonal Relevance:** Recognizing the impact of seasons on consumer preferences, Rana Harvest tailors its marketing messages and promotions to align with local seasons. For instance, during the summer, the brand may highlight the refreshing and hydrating aspects of its health-conscious products.

4. **Community Engagement Events:** To strengthen its ties with the local community and Kirana retailers, Rana Harvest actively participates in community events. In

collaboration with Kirana retailers, the brand sponsors health and wellness fairs or other community gatherings. This involvement fosters a positive brand image and establishes Rana Harvest as an integral part of the local community.

5. **Collaborative Promotions:** Rana Harvest collaborates with Kirana retailers to design promotions that specifically cater to the preferences of the local consumer base. This could include exclusive discounts or bundled offers that align with the purchasing behaviors of the community.

6. **Local Influencer Partnerships:** To amplify its reach, RanaHarvest engages with local influencers or community leaders who hold sway over the target demographic. These influencers may endorse the brand through social media, local events, or other channels, effectively leveraging their credibility within the community.

By adopting these localized marketing strategies, Rana Harvest not only showcases its commitment to understanding and respecting the local community but also ensures that its products seamlessly integrate into the Kirana retail landscape. This approach enhances the brand's visibility, builds trust among Kirana retailers and consumers, and contributes to the overall success of RanaHarvest in the local market.

4. Efficient Supply Chain

Maintaining a streamlined and efficient supply chain is paramount. Brands need to minimize disruptions, ensuring consistent product availability to meet the demands of Kirana retailers and their customers.

Certainly, let's explore the concept of "Efficient Supply Chain" in a way that resonates with an author's style, using the example of "RanaHarvest," a consumer goods brand specializing in health-conscious products. **Example:** In the intricate dance between production and distribution, RanaHarvest understands the significance of maintaining an efficient supply chain, especially when dealing with Kirana retailers. Here's how the brand ensures the seamless flow of its health-conscious products from production to Kirana store shelves: Examples are

1. **Streamlined Production Processes:** RanaHarvest invests in optimizing its production workflows. By implementing modern manufacturing techniques and technology, the brand ensures that its health-conscious products are produced with precision and in a timely manner. This streamlining not only improves overall efficiency but also reduces the likelihood of delays in meeting Kirana retailers' demands.

2. **Timely Inventory Management:** Recognizing the limited space in Kirana stores, RanaHarvest places a premium on efficient inventory management. The brand employs advanced technologies to track product movement, monitor stock levels, and anticipate demand patterns. This foresight allows the brand to maintain optimal inventory levels, ensuring Kirana retailers consistently have the products they need to meet customer demands.

3. **Collaboration with Logistics Partners:** RanaHarvest establishes strong collaborations with logistics partners who specialize in reaching Kirana retailers. These partnerships are crucial for ensuring that the health-conscious products navigate the complex web of

distribution networks, reaching Kirana stores on time and in pristine condition.

4. **Minimizing Disruptions:** Understanding the challenges posed by disruptions in the supply chain, RanaHarvest adopts proactive measures to minimize these disruptions. This includes contingency planning, alternate sourcing strategies, and constant communication with distributors and logistics partners to address any potential issues swiftly.

5. **Consistent Product Availability:** RanaHarvest places a high priority on consistent product availability. The brand aims to avoid situations where Kirana retailers face shortages of popular health-conscious products. This commitment not only enhances the brand's reliability but also strengthens the trust between RanaHarvest and Kirana retailers.

6. **Flexibility in Order Fulfillment:** Acknowledging the dynamic nature of Kirana retail, RanaHarvest offers flexibility in order fulfillment. The brand understands that Kirana retailers may have specific preferences or requirements, and it strives to accommodate these needs to the best of its ability. This flexibility fosters a collaborative partnership that goes beyond a transactional supplier-retailer relationship.

In essence, RanaHarvest's commitment to maintaining an efficient supply chain is not just about moving products from point A to point B. It's a meticulous orchestration that involves understanding the unique challenges of Kirana retail, adapting to local dynamics, and ensuring a steady and reliable flow of health-conscious products into the hands of consumers. This dedication to efficiency serves as a cornerstone in RanaHarvest's successful collaboration with Kirana retailers

5. Educational Initiatives:

Conducting educational initiatives is essential. Brands should organize training sessions for Kirana retailers, focusing on product benefits, usage, and effective marketing techniques. This builds confidence in the brand and its offerings.

"Educational Initiatives" become the guiding light for brands like RanaHarvest to empower Kirana retailers with knowledge, ensuring a harmonious partnership. Picture this scenario where RanaHarvest, a brand committed to health-conscious products, takes the lead in educating Kirana retailers:

Example:*RanaHarvest believes that knowledge is not just power; it's the cornerstone of a flourishing partnership with Kirana retailers. Here's how the brand unfolds its educational initiatives:*

1. **Product Knowledge Workshops:** RanaHarvest kickstarts a series of engaging workshops specifically tailored for Kirana retailers. These sessions delve deep into the benefits, usage, and unique selling points of the brand's health-conscious products. Imagine a gathering where Kirana retailers actively participate, gaining insights that go beyond the surface-level understanding of product features. These workshops create a shared understanding, transforming Kirana retailers into confident advocates for RanaHarvest.

2. **Effective Merchandising Techniques:** Recognizing the limited space within a Kirana store, RanaHarvest extends its educational initiatives to focus on merchandising strategies. The brand collaborates with Kirana retailers to impart skills in creating eye-catching

displays and optimizing shelf space. This hands-on approach equips retailers with the art of showcasing RanaHarvest's health-conscious products in a way that captivates the attention of health-conscious consumers.

3. **Marketing Tactics for Kirana Retail:** RanaHarvest understands that effective marketing is a shared responsibility. Through educational initiatives, the brand equips Kirana retailers with marketing tactics tailored to the local community. Picture Kirana retailers gaining insights into crafting compelling messages, leveraging local events, and engaging with customers. This collaborative learning process not only benefits RanaHarvest but also strengthens the overall marketing ecosystem within Kirana retail.

4. **Consumer Interaction Techniques:** The brand goes a step further by organizing training sessions on effective consumer interaction. Kirana retailers, armed with product knowledge, learn how to communicate the health benefits of RanaHarvest's offerings to consumers. This not only enhances the customer's shopping experience but also contributes to building trust between the retailer and the brand.

5. **Digital Literacy for Kirana Retail:** Recognizing the evolving retail landscape, RanaHarvest extends its educational initiatives to include digital literacy. Kirana retailers are guided through the integration of technology tools for inventory management, ordering processes, and even basic online presence. Imagine Kirana retailers confidently navigating digital platforms, ensuring they remain competitive in the changing retail environment.

Thus, RanaHarvest's commitment to educational initiatives goes beyond transactional benefits. It's a strategic investment in building a knowledgeable, skilled, and empowered network of Kirana retailers. Through these initiatives, RanaHarvest doesn't just sell products; it fosters a community of informed partners, ensuring a sustainable and mutually beneficial journey in the vibrant tapestry of Kirana retail.

6. Customized Merchandising:

Providing customizable merchandising solutions is crucial in optimizing limited store space effectively. Brands should collaborate with Kirana retailers to create tailored displays that attract local consumers.

examples of brands that have implemented effective strategies under the "Customized Merchandising" umbrella:

1. **Seasonal Health Corner by Himalaya Wellness:***Scenario:* Himalaya Wellness collaborates with Kirana retailers to establish a "Seasonal Health Corner." During the winter season, this dedicated space features Himalaya's immune-boosting products, herbal teas, and wellness supplements. The display incorporates winter-themed visuals and informative materials. *Brand Impact:* Himalaya Wellness optimizes limited store space, offering products aligned with seasonal health needs and reinforcing its commitment to holistic well-being.

2. **Local Wellness Fest Displays by Patanjali Ayurved:***Scenario:* Patanjali Ayurved identifies local wellness festivals and collaborates with Kirana retailers to design captivating displays. These booths showcase a diverse range of Ayurvedic products, including herbal supplements, skincare, and nutrition. Live demonstrations and interactive elements engage festival

attendees. *Brand Impact:* Patanjali Ayurved strengthens its local presence, positioning itself as a brand deeply rooted in traditional wellness practices and actively participating in community events.

3. **DIY Healthy Recipe Center by NutriChoice (Britannia):***Scenario:* NutriChoice, a brand under Britannia, partners with Kirana retailers to create a "DIY Healthy Recipe Center" within the store. The section features visually appealing recipe cards using NutriChoice products, strategically placed near relevant product sections. *Brand Impact:* NutriChoice becomes synonymous with practical and health-conscious culinary choices, leveraging Kirana retailers as influencers promoting nutritious recipes.

4. **Wellness Zone for Quick Grabs by Kellogg's Special K:***Scenario:* Kellogg's Special K collaborates with Kirana retailers to introduce a "Wellness Zone" near the checkout counter. This compact display features grab-and-go health snacks, nutritional bars, and hydration options targeting individuals seeking convenient wellness options. *Brand Impact:* Kellogg's Special K ensures visibility at a crucial touchpoint, encouraging last-minute purchases and reinforcing the brand's commitment to accessible and mindful eating.

5. **Community Health Challenges Display by Dabur Chyawanprash:***Scenario:* Dabur, known for its Ayurvedic products, collaborates with Kirana retailers to launch a "Community Health Challenge." The store features a display showcasing Dabur Chyawanprash and related products tailored for the challenge, inviting consumers to participate for improved immunity. *Brand Impact:* Dabur not only sells products but actively engages in a community-driven health initiative,

fostering a positive association with Kirana retailers as contributors to the community's well-being.

These examples illustrate how well-known brands implement customized merchandising strategies, creating tailored displays that resonate with local consumers through seasonal relevance, community engagement, and practical health solutions.

7. Collaboration with Distributors: Establishing a collaborative relationship with distributors is vital. Brands should work closely with them to streamline the onboarding process and ensure timely product delivery to Kirana retailers.

Example: Coca-Cola's Collaborative Distribution Approach

Coca-Cola, a global beverage giant, has been known for its innovative collaborations with distributors to enhance the availability and visibility of its products, including engagement with Kirana retailers.

How it worked:

1. **Localized Distribution Partnerships:** Coca-Cola collaborated with local distributors who have strong networks and relationships with Kirana retailers. These distributors understand the local market dynamics and the preferences of Kirana stores in their respective regions.

2. **Tailored Product Assortment:** Through collaboration, Coca-Cola worked with distributors to tailor product assortments based on the demand and preferences of Kirana retailers and their customer base. This ensured that the right products were stocked, minimizing the risk of overstocking or understocking.

3. **Joint Merchandising Efforts:** Coca-Cola engaged in joint merchandising efforts with distributors to create visually appealing displays within Kirana stores. This included point-of-sale materials, promotional signage, and strategically placed refrigeration units to optimize product visibility.

4. **Training and Support:** Collaborative efforts extended to training programs for Kirana retailers, facilitated by Coca-Cola and its distribution partners. These sessions covered product knowledge, effective merchandising techniques, and strategies to boost sales.

Brand Impact:

- **Enhanced Distribution Efficiency:** By collaborating closely with distributors, Coca-Cola ensured a more efficient and targeted distribution network, reaching Kirana retailers in a way that aligned with their unique requirements.

- **Improved Visibility and Availability:** Joint merchandising efforts resulted in improved visibility and availability of Coca-Cola products in Kirana stores. This collaborative approach contributed to better shelf space and increased consumer accessibility.

- **Strengthened Relationships:** The collaborative model helped build stronger relationships between Coca-Cola, distributors, and Kirana retailers. The brand's commitment to working closely with local partners demonstrated a vested interest in the success of Kirana retailers.

This example illustrates how a global brand like Coca-Cola embraced a collaborative distribution strategy, recognizing the significance of working hand-in-hand with distributors to effectively reach and serve the Kirana retail ecosystem.

8. Incentivize Retailers:

Motivating Kirana retailers through attractive incentives such as discounts, promotional schemes, or exclusive deals is essential. This fosters a sense of partnership and encourages retailers to prioritize the brand.

1. **Volume Discounts:***Example:* FMCG companies often provide volume-based discounts to retailers based on the quantity of products purchased. This encourages retailers to stock more of the brand's products.
2. **Performance Bonuses:***Example:* Some electronics brands offer performance bonuses to retailers who achieve specific sales targets. This creates motivation for retailers to actively promote and sell the brand's products.
3. **Merchandising Support:***Example:* Clothing brands may offer free merchandising materials, such as display racks or mannequins, to retailers who prominently showcase their products. This helps enhance the brand's visibility in-store.
4. **Training Programs:***Example:* Technology companies often organize training sessions for retailers on the features and benefits of their products. Retailers completing these programs might receive incentives like vouchers or additional marketing support.
5. **Co-Op Advertising Funds:***Example:* Some beverage brands allocate co-op advertising funds to retailers who actively promote the brand. This could involve sharing the costs of local advertising campaigns.

6. **Exclusive Promotions:***Example:* Cosmetic brands might offer exclusive promotions or early access to new products for retailers who consistently feature and promote their brand.

7. **Extended Payment Terms:** *Example:* Certain manufacturers provide extended payment terms to retailers who meet specific criteria, such as maintaining a certain inventory level or participating in joint marketing efforts.

8. **Reward Points Program:***Example:* A consumer electronics brand may have a reward points program where retailers earn points for every purchase, which can be redeemed for gifts, discounts, or other incentives.

9. **In-Store Displays and Signage:** Apparel brands might offer incentives for retailers who invest in creating visually appealing in-store displays and signage that showcase their products effectively.

10. **Access to Exclusive Events:** Luxury brands may provide retailers with invitations to exclusive events or product launches as incentives for achieving sales milestones.

9. Technology Integration: Facilitating easy-to-use technology solutions is pivotal. Brands should provide Kirana retailers with tools for efficient inventory management, ordering, and sales tracking to enhance overall operational efficiency. This should be done through eB2B platforms like Shopkirana (Direct), Jumbotail and likewise supply chain aggregators. Individual brand will not leave the impact of technology integration at Retailer's end but they can manage their in-App technology in such a way which can integrate with the Distributors and C&F or Super Stockiest for timely replenishment.

10. Consumer Feedback Loop: Creating a consumer feedback loop is beneficial. Sharing positive consumer reviews with Kirana retailers highlights the product's impact, reinforcing its value and market acceptance.

11. Sustainable Packaging: Emphasizing sustainable packaging aligns with the growing environmental consciousness. Kirana retailers, often rooted in their communities, appreciate eco-friendly practices, making this a significant factor in product acceptance.

Brands embracing sustainable packaging contribute to environmental consciousness and align with the growing trend of eco-friendly practices. Here are a few examples:

1. **Unilever's Sustainable Living Brands**: Unilever, a global consumer goods company, has committed to making all its packaging recyclable, reusable, or compostable by 2025. Brands under Unilever, such as Dove and Ben & Jerry's, are actively working towards sustainable packaging solutions.

2. **Procter & Gamble's Ambition 2030**: P&G has set ambitious goals for sustainable packaging under its "Ambition 2030" initiative. The company aims to make 100% of its packaging recyclable or reusable by 2030. P&G recognizes the importance of sustainable practices in the eyes of consumers and aims to lead in this area.

3. **Coca-Cola's World Without Waste:** Coca-Cola has committed to a "World Without Waste" vision, focusing on a circular economy for its packaging. The company aims to collect and recycle the equivalent of every bottle or can it sells globally by 2030. This initiative emphasizes the responsibility brands bear in managing their packaging waste.

4. **L'Oréal's Sharing Beauty with All** : L'Oréal, a major player in the beauty industry, is committed to sustainable packaging through its "Sharing Beauty with All" program. The company is working to reduce the environmental impact of its packaging, including increasing the use of recycled materials and promoting eco-design.

5. **Nestlé's Packaging Innovation:** Nestlé has been investing in innovative packaging solutions to reduce its environmental footprint. The company is exploring materials like paper for packaging and has set a target to make 100% of its packaging recyclable or reusable by 2025.

These examples showcase how leading brands across various industries are prioritizing sustainable packaging practices. Embracing eco-friendly packaging not only aligns with global environmental goals but also resonates positively with consumers and, by extension, Kirana retailers who increasingly appreciate and promote environmentally conscious products.

12. Market Trends Awareness: Keeping Kirana retailers informed about market trends is crucial. Brands should act as valuable partners, providing insights that enable retailers to offer products in line with current consumer demands.

Brands staying attuned to market trends play a pivotal role in supporting Kirana retailers' efforts to meet consumer demands. Here are examples illustrating this strategy:

1. **Apple's Innovation in Smartphones:** Apple consistently demonstrates awareness of market trends in the

technology sector. The introduction of new iPhone models with advanced features aligns with evolving consumer preferences. This approach ensures that Apple products remain in demand, reflecting an understanding of the market's dynamic nature.

2. **Fast Fashion Brands Responding to Style Trends:** Fast fashion brands like Zara and H&M excel in tracking and responding to rapidly changing fashion trends. Their ability to quickly produce and stock items that align with current styles ensures that Kirana retailers offering fashion products can cater to the latest preferences of their consumers.

3. **Beyond Meat's Plant-Based Products:** Beyond Meat, a pioneer in plant-based meat alternatives, exemplifies market trends awareness. As consumer preferences shift towards sustainable and plant-based diets, Beyond Meat's innovative products align with this trend. Kirana retailers stocking these products can tap into the rising demand for sustainable food options.

4. **Tesla's Electric Vehicles in the Automotive Sector:** Tesla's success in the automotive industry is attributed to its awareness of the market trend towards electric vehicles. By focusing on sustainable transportation solutions, Tesla has positioned itself at the forefront of an evolving automotive landscape. Kirana retailers involved in electric vehicle accessories or services can benefit from such trends.

5. **Streaming Services Adapting to Digital Consumption:** Streaming platforms like Netflix and Spotify have recognized the market trend of digital content consumption. By offering on-demand streaming services, these brands cater to the changing preferences of consumers who prefer digital entertainment. Kirana

retailers providing internet-related products can align with this trend.

These examples highlight how brands that proactively stay informed about market trends can assist Kirana retailers in offering products that resonate with consumer preferences. This approach not only ensures the relevance of products on Kirana shelves but also contributes to the adaptability and competitiveness of both the brands and the retailers in the ever-evolving market landscape.

13. Exclusive Launch Events: Organizing exclusive launch events adds significance to the brand. Creating a sense of exclusivity around the product enhances its perceived value, capturing the attention and interest of Kirana retailers.

In the FMCG sector, exclusive launch events can significantly impact brand visibility and consumer engagement. While the FMCG industry traditionally relies on mass distribution, exclusive events add a layer of excitement and anticipation. Here are examples from the Indian FMCG landscape:

1. **Patanjali's Product Launch Events:** Patanjali, a prominent FMCG brand in India, has organized exclusive launch events for various products in its portfolio, including wellness and personal care items. These events attract media attention and create a buzz around the new offerings, driving consumer interest.

2. **Hindustan Unilever's Premium Product Launches:** Hindustan Unilever (HUL), a leading FMCG company, occasionally hosts exclusive launch events for premium or innovative products. For instance, the launch of a new skincare range or a unique food product might be

accompanied by an exclusive event, elevating the product's perceived value.

3. **Nestlé's Special Edition Launches:** Nestlé, known for its diverse range of food and beverage products, has utilized exclusive launch events for special editions or innovative product variants. These events serve to showcase the uniqueness of the products, attracting attention from both consumers and retailers.

4. **ITC's New Brand Introductions:** ITC, with its presence in FMCG segments such as food, personal care, and lifestyle, has employed exclusive launch events for introducing new brands or expanding product lines. These events contribute to building brand recognition and fostering retailer interest.

5. **Dabur's Health and Wellness Product Launches:** Dabur, a major player in health and wellness products, has organized exclusive events for the launch of specific health-focused products. These events highlight the brand's commitment to well-being, capturing the attention of Kirana retailers and consumers alike.

These examples illustrate how FMCG brands in India leverage exclusive launch events to create a memorable introduction for their products. Kirana retailers partnering with such brands can benefit from the increased visibility and consumer excitement generated by these events, contributing to a positive and dynamic retail environment

14. Financial Assistance:

Financial assistance or credit facilities eases the burden on Kirana retailers. This fosters long-term partnerships by demonstrating a commitment to the success of the retailer. Now a days various NBFC and Micro finance startups coming up with various financial products in the form of channel funding which can leverage the need of facilitating credit to retailers.

Financial assistance plays a crucial role in establishing strong and enduring partnerships between brands and Kirana retailers. Several brands, especially in the FMCG sector, have implemented financial assistance programs to support retailers in various aspects of their business. Additionally, Non-Banking Financial Companies (NBFCs) have emerged as key players in providing channel funding, with brands often leveraging their corporate guarantees. Here are examples showcasing how financial assistance initiatives, including those involving NBFCs, have been employed:

1. **Procter & Gamble's Channel Funding Programs:** Procter & Gamble (P&G) has implemented channel funding programs to assist Kirana retailers associated with its distribution network. These programs may include financial support for marketing initiatives, store improvements, or specific promotional activities, contributing to the retailer's overall business growth.

2. **ITC's Trade Schemes and Credit Support:** ITC, operating in multiple FMCG categories, has introduced trade schemes and credit support programs for Kirana retailers. These initiatives involve offering discounts, extended credit periods, or financial incentives tied to sales performance, enhancing the retailer's profitability.

3. **Hindustan Unilever's Distributor Financing Programs:** Hindustan Unilever (HUL) has initiated distributor financing programs that indirectly benefit Kirana retailers. By supporting distributors in managing their finances, HUL ensures a smoother supply chain, leading to better service for Kirana outlets and

potentially offering financial assistance directly to retailers.

4. **Nestlé's Flexible Payment Terms**: Nestlé has implemented flexible payment terms for Kirana retailers, allowing them to manage their cash flow more effectively. This form of financial assistance contributes to the retailer's financial stability and creates a positive partnership dynamic.

5. **Coca-Cola's Equipment Financing Initiatives**: Coca-Cola, operating in the beverage industry, has introduced equipment financing initiatives for retailers. This assistance includes financing options for acquiring refrigeration units or vending machines, enhancing the overall store infrastructure.

6. **Marico's Distributor Credit Programs**: Marico, known for its hair care and skincare products, has established distributor credit programs that indirectly benefit Kirana retailers. These programs ensure that distributors can extend credit to retailers, facilitating smooth business operations.

7. **Dabur's Support for Modernization**: Dabur has provided financial support to Kirana retailers looking to modernize their stores. This assistance may include funding for store renovations, technology adoption, or other enhancements that align with changing consumer preferences.

8. **Colgate-Palmolive's Working Capital Support**: Colgate-Palmolive has implemented working capital support programs for its distributors, ensuring a stable financial ecosystem that positively impacts Kirana retailers through consistent product availability.

9. **Britannia's Retailer Development Funds**: Britannia Industries has established retailer development funds

to assist Kirana retailers in marketing and promotional activities. This financial support aims to enhance the visibility and sales performance of Britannia products in Kirana stores.

NBFCs Providing Channel Funding:

- **Khatabook Capital:** Khatabook Capital is a notable NBFC offering financial solutions, including channel funding, to retailers. Brands can collaborate with Khatabook Capital to extend financial assistance to Kirana retailers, leveraging their corporate guarantee.
- **OkCredit Finance:** OkCredit Finance provides financial services tailored for retailers, including channel funding. Brands partnering with OkCredit Finance can enhance their financial support programs for Kirana retailers.
- **Snapbizz Finance:** Snapbizz Finance specializes in providing financial support to retailers in the FMCG sector. Brands can utilize Snapbizz Finance to extend channel funding to Kirana retailers, ensuring a robust financial ecosystem.
- **Capital Float:** Capital Float is an NBFC that offers flexible financing solutions to small and medium-sized enterprises (SMEs), including retailers. Brands can explore partnerships with Capital Float to extend financial support to Kirana retailers.
- **Lendingkart:** Lendingkart provides working capital loans and financial assistance to businesses, including retailers. Brands can collaborate with Lendingkart to facilitate channel funding for Kirana retailers.
- **Indifi:** Indifi is a platform that connects businesses with suitable lenders, offering specialized financial solutions.

Brands can leverage Indifi to channel funds and support Kirana retailers in their network.

- **FlexiLoans:** FlexiLoans specializes in providing quick and flexible business loans to SMEs, including retailers. Brands looking to enhance their financial assistance programs can consider collaborating with FlexiLoans.
- **InCred:** InCred is a diversified NBFC offering various financial products, including business loans. Brands can explore InCred's offerings to extend financial support and channel funding to Kirana retailers.
- **NeoGrowth:** NeoGrowth provides innovative lending solutions, particularly focused on retailers. Brands can partner with NeoGrowth to facilitate channel funding for Kirana retailers, supporting their business growth.
- **Aye Finance:** Aye Finance caters to the financial needs of micro and small businesses, including retailers. Brands can explore collaboration with Aye Finance to enhance financial assistance programs for Kirana retailers.
- **MSME Schemes by Banks:** Many traditional banks offer specific schemes and financial products tailored for Micro, Small, and Medium Enterprises (MSMEs), including retailers. Brands can work in collaboration with banks to extend financial support to Kirana retailers through these schemes.

It's essential for brands to assess the specific financial needs of Kirana retailers and choose a channel funding partner that aligns with their objectives and the retailers' requirements. Collaborating with these financial institutions can contribute to the overall financial health and sustainability of Kirana retailers within the brand's network.

15. Brand Loyalty Programs:

Introducing loyalty programs for Kirana retailers is a strategic move. Recognizing and rewarding consistent support and sales performance strengthens the bond between the brand and the retailer. In the fast-moving consumer goods (FMCG) sector, building strong relationships with Kirana retailers is paramount for brand success. Brand loyalty programs serve as a strategic tool to engage and incentivize retailers, fostering a sense of partnership and commitment. Here are insights into how several FMCG companies implement brand loyalty programs to strengthen their ties with Kirana retailers:

1. **Godrej Consumer Products Limited (GCPL):** GCPL focuses on exclusive promotions, point-based reward systems, and training programs to enhance the visibility and sales of its products in Kirana stores. The loyalty initiatives are designed to recognize and appreciate the contributions of retailers.
2. **Unilever (HUL):** HUL implements innovative loyalty programs that often include tiered rewards, marketing support, and exclusive offers. These programs aim to incentivize retailers to stock and actively promote HUL products, fostering a mutually beneficial partnership.
3. **Nirma Limited:** Nirma's loyalty initiatives encompass financial incentives, co-branded promotional materials, and periodic engagement activities. These efforts aim to create a positive and collaborative environment, encouraging retailers to prioritize Nirma products.
4. **Parle Products:** Parle's loyalty programs offer rewards for achieving sales targets, participation in brand promotions, and exclusive access to new product launches. These initiatives are designed to motivate retailers to actively promote and showcase Parle

products.

5. **Jyothy Labs:** Jyothy Labs engages Kirana retailers through loyalty programs featuring incentives for promoting products, participating in training sessions, and collaborating on localized marketing efforts. These initiatives strengthen the partnership between the brand and retailers.

6. **Emami Limited:** Emami emphasizes strong relationships with Kirana retailers through loyalty programs that include point-based rewards, financial incentives, and co-marketing opportunities. These initiatives encourage active promotion of Emami products in Kirana stores.

7. **McCormick & Company (Vadilal):** McCormick's loyalty programs for Kirana retailers may include rewards for achieving sales targets, merchandising support, and collaborative efforts to enhance product visibility. These initiatives aim to build a collaborative approach to sales and promotion.

8. **Hershey India:** Hershey India implements loyalty programs to engage Kirana retailers in promoting its confectionery and chocolate products. These programs feature incentives for meeting sales goals, participating in brand campaigns, and receiving marketing support.

9. **Everest Spices:** Everest Spices engages Kirana retailers through loyalty programs offering incentives for promoting and stocking its products. These initiatives contribute to increased sales and brand visibility in Kirana stores.

These brand loyalty programs play a crucial role in fostering dynamic and mutually beneficial collaborations between FMCG companies and Kirana retailers. Through incentives, recognition, and collaborative support, these programs contribute to the overall success of both parties in the competitive FMCG landscape.

16. Digital Presence Support:

Assisting Kirana retailers in establishing a digital presence is crucial in the evolving retail landscape. Brands should provide guidance and support to ensure retailers remain competitive online.

- Establishing a digital presence is crucial for Kirana retailers to remain competitive in the modern retail landscape.
- FMCG brands understand the significance of guiding Kirana retailers through the process of digitalization.
- Support includes creating online profiles, optimizing product listings, and leveraging social media for increased visibility.

17. Localized Language Support:

Offering marketing materials and support in local languages facilitates better communication and understanding between brands and Kirana retailers. This cultural sensitivity strengthens the brand-retailer relationship.

18. Quality Assurance Initiatives:

Implementing robust quality assurance programs is fundamental. Building trust and confidence in the brand's products is essential for Kirana retailers to recommend and sell them to their customers.

19. Collaborative Advertising:

Engaging in joint advertising efforts benefits both brands and Kirana retailers. Sharing the cost and benefits of promotional activities strengthens the brand's visibility in the local market. This is utilized by retailers to engage their local customer base. Brands can create brochures containing a personalized message from the retailer, along with special offers that highlight the value for money. This approach encourages a call to action, effectively prompting an increase in customer footfall

20. Flexible Return Policies:

Implementing flexible return policies addresses Kirana retailers' concerns about slow-moving inventory. This flexibility helps build trust and encourages retailers to experiment with new products.

- Kirana retailers often grapple with concerns related to slow-moving inventory, product expiration, and market fluctuations.
- Rigid return policies can discourage retailers from experimenting with new products, hindering the introduction of innovative offerings.

Occasionally, these policies may not align with the retailer's preferences, leading to hesitance in onboarding. Brands need to address this issue by implementing robust expiry management and guarantee policies. Assuring retailers that expired or unsold products can be returned or replaced establishes a sense of belongingness and ownership. Such a commitment fosters respect from the retailer, creating a positive and mutually beneficial relationship.

21. Community Engagement:

Participating in community events and supporting local causes is impactful. This fosters a positive brand image among Kirana retailers and their consumers, enhancing the brand's reputation.

Example: Rana & Co, a renowned consumer goods company, took an active role in a health and wellness fair organized by the local community in collaboration with Kirana retailers. The brand not only sponsored the event but also set up a booth showcasing their range of health-conscious products.

In addition, Rana & Co collaborated with Kirana retailers to conduct informative sessions on healthy living and nutritional choices. They distributed pamphlets in the local language, educating consumers about the benefits of Rana & Co's products.

Simultaneously, Rana & Co supported a local charity initiative by donating a percentage of their sales during the fair to a community healthcare program. This dual engagement not only enhanced Rana & Co's reputation among Kirana retailers but also left a positive impression on consumers, establishing the brand as one that genuinely cares about local well-being.

22. Health and Wellness Focus:

Emphasizing health and wellness benefits in product offerings aligns with the increasing consumer focus on well-being. This resonates well with Kirana retailers catering to health-conscious communities. Here are some examples.

a. ***Introduction of Organic Snack Range:*** *Rana & Co recognized the growing trend of health-conscious consumers in the community served by Kirana retailers. In response, they introduced a new line of organic snacks, free from artificial preservatives and additives. The packaging prominently displayed nutritional information, emphasizing the health benefits. Kirana retailers, understanding the preferences of their health-conscious customers, welcomed the new product line, and it quickly gained popularity among the community.*

b. ***Collaboration on Nutritional Workshops:*** *To further emphasize health and wellness, Rana & Co collaborated with Kirana retailers to organize nutritional workshops in the local community. These workshops focused on promoting balanced diets and the benefits of incorporating Rana & Co's range of nutritious products. Kirana retailers actively participated, incorporating the gained knowledge into their interactions with customers. This joint initiative not only strengthened the brand's association with health but also positioned Kirana retailers as advocates for the well-being of their community.*

c. ***Health-Conscious Recipe Campaign:*** *Rana & Co initiated a campaign promoting health-conscious recipes using their products. They provided recipe cards to Kirana retailers, encouraging them to share these with their customers. The recipes highlighted the nutritional value of ingredients, aligning with the health and wellness focus. Kirana retailers, acting as influencers within their communities, actively promoted these recipes, fostering a positive association between Rana & Co's products and a healthy lifestyle in the eyes of* the consumers.

23. Regular Communication Channels:

Establishing regular communication channels is essential for addressing concerns, gathering feedback, and providing updates to Kirana retailers. This ongoing dialogue strengthens the brand-retailer relationship. Examples are:

a. *Recognizing the importance of open communication, Rana & Co implemented a robust system of regular communication channels with Kirana retailers. They established a dedicated helpline and email support, ensuring accessibility for retailers to address concerns or seek assistance promptly.*

b. *In addition, Rana & Co organized monthly virtual feedback sessions, inviting Kirana retailers to share insights, challenges, and suggestions. These interactive sessions not only provided a platform for retailers to voice their concerns but also allowed Rana & Co to gather valuable feedback for continuous improvement.*

c. *Moreover, Rana & Co initiated a monthly newsletter sent to Kirana retailers, featuring product updates, promotional offers, and industry trends. This proactive communication strategy kept retailers well-informed and engaged.*

d. *By fostering this ongoing dialogue, Rana & Co not only addressed concerns promptly but also demonstrated a commitment to a transparent and collaborative relationship with Kirana retailers, ultimately strengthening the bond between the brand and its retail partners.*

24. Trade Shows Participation:

Actively participating in trade shows and exhibitions allows Kirana retailers to experience and understand the brand firsthand. This direct interaction aids in building trust and interest.

25. Technology Training Programs:

Offering training programs on utilizing technology for inventory management is essential. Helping Kirana retailers adapt to modern retail practices ensures efficiency and competitiveness.

26. Market Expansion Support:

Supporting Kirana retailers in market expansion efforts demonstrates a commitment to mutual growth. Brands should actively contribute to the retailer's efforts to reach new customers.

27. E-commerce Integration: Facilitating integration with e-commerce platforms is strategic. Enabling Kirana retailers to tap into online sales opportunities broadens the brand's reach beyond the physical store. In this process few startups are taking such initiatives, among are Khatabook, Snapbizz, Okcredit and many more.

28. Social Media Engagement:

Leveraging social media to create awareness and buzz around the brand is essential. Involving Kirana retailers in online marketing efforts expands the brand's digital presence.

29. Regular Performance Reviews:

Conducting regular performance reviews with Kirana retailers is a proactive approach. Assessing sales patterns, identifying challenges, and strategizing for improvement ensures a dynamic and adaptive partnership. These are :

h. ***Monthly Sales Analytics Meeting:*** *Rana & Co conducts a monthly virtual meeting with Kirana retailers to analyze sales data. Together, they review sales patterns, identify top-performing products, and discuss strategies to enhance overall revenue. This collaborative approach allows for real-time adjustments and ensures the product mix aligns with consumer demand.*

a. ***Quarterly Operational Efficiency Assessment:*** *Every quarter, Rana & Co assesses the operational efficiency of Kirana retailers. The review covers inventory management, order fulfillment, and customer service. By identifying operational challenges, Rana & Co can* *provide targeted support and resources to streamline processes, fostering a more efficient partnership.*

j. ***Seasonal Product Performance Analysis:*** *Recognizing the impact of seasons on consumer preferences, Rana & Co conducts a seasonal product performance analysis with Kirana retailers. This review helps anticipate trends, optimize inventory for specific seasons, and develop targeted marketing strategies to capitalize on seasonal demand fluctuations.*

k. ***Customer Satisfaction Surveys:*** *Periodic customer satisfaction surveys are conducted in collaboration with Kirana retailers. Rana & Co seeks feedback on product satisfaction, packaging, and overall shopping experience. This approach ensures that the brand addresses any concerns promptly, enhancing customer satisfaction and loyalty.*

ax. ***Training and Skill Enhancement Sessions:*** *In addition to sales performance reviews, Rana & Co organizes regular training sessions for Kirana retailers. These sessions focus on enhancing sales skills, product knowledge, and customer engagement. The performance review includes an assessment of the effectiveness of these training initiatives in improving the retailer's overall performance and customer interactions.*

By implementing these varied approaches to regular performance reviews, Rana & Co ensures a comprehensive evaluation of the partnership with Kirana retailers, leading to a dynamic and adaptive collaboration.

30. Case Studies and Success Stories:

Sharing case studies and success stories of other brands successfully collaborating with Kirana retailers provides real-world examples. This builds confidence and showcases the potential benefits of the partnership.

In the complex world of retail, Kirana retailers play a crucial role, holding significant sway in shaping how brands are perceived. With a constant stream of 10-15 new brands seeking attention daily, time management becomes a critical skill for these retailers. Over the past 15 years, the retail landscape has transformed with the introduction of new products, the rise of retail chains, and local brands challenging national players.

Once the driving force in introducing consumers to new products, Kirana retailers now face challenges from offline giants like Dmart, Jiomart, Local hyperlocal chains and quick commerce platforms, leading to a decline in their enthusiasm for exploring new brands. Distributors are also less motivated due to the shrinking business of retailers.

For new brands aiming to establish themselves in Kirana retail, the challenge lies in convincing distributors, wholesalers, and retailers to showcase their products. The exploration of Direct-to-Consumer (D2C) as a direct consumer outreach avenue raises questions about scalability and impact, recognizing the indispensable role of Kirana retailers.

Looking ahead five years, it seems brands will face increased struggles to secure a respected place within Kirana retail shops. In this ever-changing retail landscape, innovative strategies, adaptability, and a deep understanding of Kirana retailers' unique challenges become paramount.

The subsequent 30 remedies outlined form a comprehensive guide for brands to effectively position their products within the Kirana retail landscape. Understanding Kirana operations, adopting a data-driven approach, crafting localized marketing strategies, and maintaining an efficient supply chain are among the key strategies. Educational initiatives, collaborative efforts with distributors, and incentivizing retailers contribute to building a symbiotic relationship.

Technological integration, sustainable practices, market trend awareness, and exclusive launch events are additional pillars supporting a brand's presence. Financial assistance, loyalty programs, and digital presence support address the evolving needs of Kirana retailers. Language localization, quality assurance, collaborative advertising, and flexible return policies enhance the brand-retailer rapport.

The examples provided for health and wellness focus showcase how brands like Rana & Co can align with Kirana retailers catering to health-conscious communities. Additionally, the emphasis on regular communication channels, technology training, market expansion support, and social media engagement ensures a dynamic partnership.

Regular performance reviews, exemplified by various approaches, such as sales analytics meetings, operational efficiency assessments, and seasonal product performance analyses, signify a proactive and adaptive collaboration. Case studies and success stories serve as real-world illustrations of brands successfully navigating the Kirana retail landscape.

In conclusion, the journey to build robust relationships with Kirana retailers demands a holistic and tailored approach. By implementing these 30 strategies, brands not only navigate the complexities of the evolving retail landscape but also earn the trust of Kirana retailers, securing a prominent and enduring place in the market.

--==--

Closing Notes

As we approach the conclusion of **Kiranawala**, it becomes abundantly clear that Kirana retailers are far more than mere shopkeepers; they are the very lifeblood of India's retail ecosystem. Their resilience, adaptability, and unwavering dedication to their communities position them as irreplaceable pillars of both the economy and society. Throughout this journey, we have delved into the rich and multifaceted world of Kirana retail, exploring the humble origins of these stores and their evolution in the face of modern retail challenges. We have witnessed how Kirana retailers, often operating from modest spaces, manage to cultivate thriving centres of commerce and community. Their unique ability to blend tradition with innovation—offering personalised service while embracing technology—sets them apart in an increasingly digital world.

Kirana retailers make a significant **contribution to India's GDP and employment, comprising a substantial portion of the retail market.** Their economic influence extends beyond mere transactions, as they support local suppliers, create jobs, and stimulate economic growth at the grassroots level. In a country as diverse as India, Kirana stores are attuned to the specific needs of their communities, offering products that cater to local tastes and preferences. *Kiranawala* has shed light on the numerous challenges faced by Kirana retailers, from competition with large retail chains and e-commerce platforms to the pressing need for modernisation and technological integration. Yet, it is within these challenges that opportunities for growth and transformation lie.

Kirana retailers have displayed remarkable resilience, adjusting to changing consumer behaviours and market dynamics. By embracing technology, streamlining supply chains, and enhancing customer engagement, they can continue to flourish in the evolving retail landscape.

Technology has emerged as a transformative force for Kirana retailers. Mobile apps, point-of-sale systems, and inventory management tools have streamlined operations, boosting efficiency and enhancing the customer experience. The integration of e-commerce platforms has also opened new channels for growth, enabling Kirana stores to extend their reach to a broader customer base. Startups and corporate initiatives have played a vital role in providing the resources and expertise necessary for this digital transformation. Beyond their business acumen, Kirana retailers are also custodians of tradition and sustainability. Many have adopted eco-friendly practices, reducing plastic usage and promoting locally sourced products. Their commitment to sustainability reflects a profound sense of responsibility towards both the environment and their communities. Moreover, Kirana stores often serve as community hubs, nurturing social interactions and supporting local initiatives. Their role in fostering social cohesion and community well-being cannot be overstated.

Looking to the future, the prospects for Kirana retail are bright. *Kiranawala* has highlighted several emerging trends, such as the increasing focus on health and wellness, the rise of sustainable products, and the growing significance of personalised customer service. Kirana retailers are uniquely positioned to capitalise on these trends, leveraging their deep-rooted connections with their communities. By forging strategic collaborations, embracing innovation, and staying attuned to market shifts, they can remain relevant and prosperous. As we bring this exploration of Kirana retail to a close, it is crucial to acknowledge the collective effort required to support and uplift these small businesses. Policymakers, corporate entities, and consumers all have a role to play in ensuring the sustainability and growth of Kirana stores. By providing access to finance, technology, and training, we can empower Kirana retailers to navigate the challenges of the modern retail landscape. Consumers, too, can make a difference by choosing to support their local Kirana stores, appreciating the personalised service and sense of community they offer.

This book is a tribute to the unsung heroes of India's retail sector—the Kirana retailers. Their stories of perseverance, innovation, and community spirit inspire us all. As we celebrate their contributions, let us also commit to supporting their journey toward a brighter and more prosperous future. In closing, the spirit of Kirana retail stands as a testament to the resilience and ingenuity of small businesses. It reminds us that, even in an era of rapid change, the values of trust, community, and personalised service remain timeless. Let us continue to champion the cause of Kirana retailers, ensuring that they remain the backbone of India's retail landscape for generations to come.

Appeal to the Readers of this book

My appeal to the vast section of India's shoppers is simple yet urgent: the future of our communities and economy depends on the choices we make today. Kirana stores, the backbone of India's retail landscape, are more than just places to buy everyday essentials—they are the lifeblood of millions of families and the foundation of local economies across the country. If we, as consumers, neglect these small yet mighty businesses, we risk far more than the loss of a shopping option—we risk the very fabric of our economy.

Kirana retailers contribute significantly **to India's GDP and employment, accounting for up to 10% of the country's economic output and providing 8% of all jobs.** These figures are not mere statistics; they represent real people, real jobs, and the survival of countless families. Each purchase made at a local Kirana store supports the livelihoods of individuals, sustains small businesses, and strengthens local economies.

Some thought-provoking and impactful quotes that could resonate with the significance of Kirana retailers:

1. **"A Kirana store is not just a shop, but a lifeline to the community it serves."**
2. **"The heart of India's retail is in the hands of the Kiranawala—the unsung heroes who nourish our lives, one purchase at a time."**
3. **"Kirana retailers are the silent architects of our neighbourhoods, where trust, tradition, and service build the foundation of India's retail economy."**
4. **"In every Kirana store, there is a story of resilience, a commitment to community, and a dedication to the**

future of India's economy."

5. "The Kirana store represents the spirit of India—rooted in tradition, yet ever-evolving to meet the needs of the modern world."

6. "Supporting a Kirana store is not just a transaction; it's an investment in local prosperity and the heartbeat of India's economy."

7. "In a world that's rapidly digitalising, the Kiranawala reminds us that true customer service and community connection still thrive in the small corners of our streets."

8. "Behind every Kirana counter lies a story of hard work, dedication, and the quiet strength that sustains our local economies."

These quotes reflect the deep, symbolic importance of Kirana stores in India's economy and society, highlighting the personal and community-centered service they provide.

My heart wrote these lines in the form of a poem

Support them in your best way,
They are near to you, not far away.
In every corner, on every street,
Kirana stores make life complete.
With humble smiles and steady hands,
They serve the needs of countless lands.
From morning's light to evening's call,
They're the heart that beats for all.
Through every challenge, they stand tall,
A lifeline for the great and small.
So, when you shop, remember this,
Your Kirana store is pure bliss.
Support them now, and in the days,
For they sustain in countless ways.

They're near to you, not far at all,
The backbone of our lives—big and small.

Therefore, I urge you to make a conscious choice. By buying your daily essentials from a Kirana store, you are ensuring their continued survival. You are investing in your community, in jobs, and in the prosperity of our nation. This is not just a matter of convenience; it is a matter of survival for small businesses and for the future of India's economy. Let us stand together in support of Kirana retailers, ensuring that they remain the cornerstone of our retail ecosystem for generations to come.

--==--